India and SAARC:
Critical Issues and Challenges

Dr. Susanta Kumar Parida

GenNext Publication

Published by

GenNext Publication
5, Ansari Road
Daryaganj, New Delhi-110002
Phone: 011-47034999, 9811692060
E-mail: gennextpublication@hotmail.com

Distribution Network
gyanbooks.com
India, USA, Canada, UK, Australia, France

ISBN: 978-93-5663-178-6 (PB)

First Published, 2024

Printed at: Gyan Press, Delhi.

INDIA AND SAARC:
Critical Issues and Challenges
Author: Dr. Susanta Kumar Parida

India and SAARC:
Critical Issues and Challenges

Contents

Foreword

The South Asian Association for Regional Cooperation (SAARC), comprising eight nations, is a critical organization aimed at fostering regional cooperation and development. Since its formation in 1985, SAARC has faced challenges stemming from the diverse political, economic, and social realities of its member states. Despite its potential, the organization continues to confront several key issues that have hindered its effectiveness in promoting regional integration and progress.

The ongoing rivalry between India and Pakistan is a major obstacle to SAARC's success. While India holds significant regional influence due to its size, economy, and geographic position, the unresolved tensions between the two nations, dating back to their 1947 partition, persist. Border disputes, maritime conflicts, and external alliances, such as Sino-Bangladesh and Sino-Sri Lankan partnerships, have further eroded trust within the organization. SAARC's inability to mediate and resolve bilateral conflicts, particularly between India and Pakistan, weakens its capacity to facilitate regional cooperation.

The nuclearization of South Asia in 1998, following nuclear tests by both India and Pakistan, escalated tensions between the two countries. The 2001 Kargil conflict further heightened the threat of nuclear warfare. Terrorism, including incidents like the 2008 Mumbai attacks, has also disrupted peace and security efforts in the region. India's nuclear policy focuses on deterrence, whereas Pakistan has adopted a more aggressive approach, adding complexity to the already strained relations. Without improved ties between these two major SAARC members, the organization's effectiveness will remain limited.

This book, *India and SAARC: Critical Issues and Challenges*, offers a comprehensive examination of India's role within SAARC and its relationships with other member nations. As the largest and most influential member, India significantly shapes the future of SAARC and the broader South Asian region. However, this leadership comes with challenges, as India must navigate its national interests while promoting regional cooperation.

The book delves into India's perspective on SAARC, its bilateral relations with other member states, and the contributions it has made to the organization. It also explores the challenges India faces within the SAARC framework. Additionally, it provides policy recommendations aimed at enhancing cooperation and collaboration among member countries.

Authored by Dr. Susanta Kumar Parida, the book addresses critical concerns such as trade imbalances, security dilemmas, political tensions, and socio-economic disparities. It analyzes India's relationships with its neighbors, offering insights into how historical legacies, geopolitical strategies, and contemporary issues have influenced both cooperation and discord within SAARC. The book also contextualizes these dynamics within the broader global environment, noting the rise of new regional organizations and shifts in international diplomacy, which have further complicated SAARC's role.

For students of international relations, policymakers, and anyone interested in the region, this book provides valuable insights into the complex forces shaping South Asia's future. The analyses and reflections presented are essential for understanding the ongoing debates surrounding SAARC's effectiveness.

As SAARC continues to confront internal and external challenges, this book will serve as a catalyst for further reflection, discussion, and action toward realizing the full potential of South Asian unity.

Dr. Pramod Jaiswal
Research Director,
Nepal Institute for International Cooperation and Engagement (NIICE),
Lalitpur, Nepal
15 September 2024

Acknowledgements

This book is the result of guidance, assistance, and inspiration of several people. I am deeply grateful to all the individuals who have played a role both direct and indirect in successful completion of the book.

I am extremely grateful to Prof. Anil Kumar Mohapatra, Professor of Political Science, Fakir Mohan University, Balasore, Odisha, Prof. Radhanath Tripathy, University of Delhi and Prof. Narottam Gaan, Professor and former Head, Department of Political Science and Human Rights, Indira Gandhi National Tribal University (IGNTU), Amarkantak, Mdhya Pradesh for their valuable advices and suggestions which help me a lot for this research work.

Similarly my thanks go to Dr. Pramod Jaiswal, Research Director, Nepal Institute for International Cooperation and Engagement (NIICE), Lalitpur, Nepal for critical analysis the book and giving a nice foreword for the book.

I also acknowledge with thanks for the support provided by GenNext Publications, New Delhi.

Last, but not the least, my personal and heartfelt gratitude goes to my father Mr. Sarbeswar Parida, my mother Mrs. Manjubala Parida, my wife Dr. Anuradha Das, my son Aurosish, my brother Subharnsu, sister in law Monalisa and my sweet sister budhia for their love and support.

I am grateful that the Divine Mother has placed all of you in my life.

Dr. Susanta Kumar Parida

Chapter - 1

Genesis and Evolution of SAARC

Regionalism developed in the post-World War II era as a significant, if not dominant, phenomenon. To arrange their international relations, the critical issue for third world regionalist organisations should be to alleviate some more dysfunctional conventional ambitions of the sovereign state system. Peace and well-being are essential inputs to this order. Regional integration routes slipping off from these traditional activities are one method for the less-developed nations to progress in their direction.[1]. Thus, it is evident that regionalism can only be achieved successfully by removing excessive nationalism and seeking global peace and well-being.

A vast number of published works linked to regionalism and the international order were generated by Regional Integration Theory. These resources have been split into three sections 1. Federalism 2. Neo-functionalism and 3. Functonilasim

Federalism distinguishes from neo-functionalism because functionalism is mainly a political and legal strategy for integration and not a socio-economic one. The federalist is convinced by the supranational objective, which ranges from international to supra-national, with sufficient political legitimacy and coercive and material strength to guarantee their members' collective defence. It ensures that its federal components enjoy local authority. Global human welfare is dealt with within the regional schemes of the International Federation, much as the government in a state unit maintains peace and guarantees the good of its people.

1. Khan Feroz, H. 2008. Security Impediments to Regionalism in South Asia. Paper presented at the conference on "Does South Asia Exist? Prospects for Regionalism in South Asia". Stanford University.

However, the experience of the attempted fusion of achieved sovereignty was not successful in the post-World War II era. On the other side, the propensity to disintegration has become increasingly apparent, as shown by the Soviet Union's split into numerous separate nations. The East European experience may also be used to demonstrate the truth of this statement.

The neo-functionalist method developed around 1950 when the European coal and steel community (ECSC) unveiled a proposal to unify Europe's coal and steel markets. The idea was obviously to ensure people's well-being and was not politically and legally inclined. This theory has features comparable to those of classical theory. Classical theory hopes that the trend to conflict may be avoided via non-political forms of collaboration in shared tasks across different governments and cultures by creating a feeling of community. Both the conventional and the neo-classical approaches are essentially pluralistic and oriented towards the community, reject integration by a model of classical federalism by forces-state, understate the role of politicians, instead emphasise that technocrats are much more politically aware, although neo-functionalist technocrats, contrary to classical technocrats[1]. They believe that power and well-being cannot be long separated. Neo-functionalist E. Hass Claims that supranational represents an economical over political triumph. The supremacy of the economy has made force politics obsolete. The dominance and importance of social-welfare politics over power politics is the foundation of the integrated supranational regional organisation.

The classical functionalists, however, are skeptical of neo-functionalists' political, regional and federal goals. The classics more embrace the ECSC and Euratom communities than the European Economic Community (E.E.C), which anticipates that the E.E.C. would inevitably lead to integration in many more areas. At the same time, the former seems to be particular in function and, in nature, more restricted.

The regionalist functionalist approach is mainly characterised by the non-political functioning of the international organisation with the creation of the U.N. League." Functionalists do not accept regional federalism or neo-functionalism as the most useful or sustainable solution to the world order. They say that federalism goes alongside functionality because its coercive institutional apparatus of the state and its report on politics in

1. Maatli, W. 1999. The Logic of Regional Integration: Europe and Beyond. Cambridge: Cambridge University Press.

international relations requires state construction in a conventional sense. In response to the supranational goals of neofunctionalists, functionalism maintains that geographical exclusivism is the main feature of the regional integration approach, which is likely to hinder federalists' operational welfare flow that cannot be partition sized politically, especially in the age of globalism, by technological and economic development. The functionalism is founded on the idea that form must be based upon function, i.e. technical autonomy. The borders are defined functionally. The officials say that a functioning peace system is being developed that may reduce conflict by allowing cross-cutting loyalties, generating a feeling of security by performing a required function instead of a system of threats.

1.1 Regional organisations- Post-Second World-War Phenomena

Western Europe began the process of development of regional organisations. Its roots were primarily political, and the need to unite the capitalist nations against the communist menace was satisfied. NATO was created in 1949, and after more than 40 decades of the cold war, western Europe has succeeded not only in implementing its military deterrent but also in developing an enhanced economic integration that grew from the coal and steel community to the European financial community and is currently about to set into a more intimate unit in the years ahead. The Europeans who were interacting with the superpower, which consisted of federations of numerous constituent units (50 in the U.S. and 15 in the U.S.S.), realised an unavoidable need to galvanise into an economic force capable of dealing fairly with significant powers such as the U.S. and USSR, and with emerging new giants in Asia. The success of the E.E.C. stimulated regional integration in other areas of the globe via organisations such as the South East Asian Nations Association (ASEAN), founded in 1960, which was replaced by the Latin America Integration Association in 1980. The regional integration process in Africa may reach an intensity that could not be seen elsewhere. At the beginning of the 1980s, over 30 regional organisations were operating throughout Africa. 11 Many are young and weak. Still, they reveal the changes in Member States' political views, a desire to become less dependent than industrialised countries in the West, and an attempt at collective sovereignty.

It is a harsh fact, though, that in the third world, increasing economic and political integration has proven less helpful by regional organisations compared with the successes obtained by Western Europe, North America and Eastern Europe. The European model shows that a relative degree of balance, complementary and extent of its components are the main element that facilitates the success of a regional organisation's management of shared interests. In addition to higher economic and technical development levels and similar security views, the western European model represents a high degree of balance. Eastern Europe also saw, apart from the shared idea of ideology, a common danger to the hegemonic of a superpower to ensure the success of the original integrative institutions. In summary, shared views of threats and complementary and ideological similarities are elements that lead to East and Western European organisations and contribute to their success without question.

At the moment, to solve their economic difficulties, third-world nations rely on the industrialised West. Including a tactically but economically unenviable area is undoubtedly more likely to be susceptible to external pressure that impedes the integration process. The primary aim of third-world nations should be to remove from their international relations the more dysfunctional conventional functions of a sovereign state system. If you need to state here, it cannot be an end to promoting regional integration. Such integration must serve mainly the purpose of domestic economic growth and, in particular, poverty reduction. Today, most third-world nations have joined the NIEO inside the North-South Dialog and demand outward redistribution of internal changes.[1]. You notice that bilateral Cooperation with N.N.C. and international organisations have not indeed addressed their poverty issues. It is generally believed that all kinds of regionalism should contribute to the fundamental change of global society.

1.2 Regional Integration and South Asia

The idea of South Asian regional integration is a record wave of regionalism, as it is seen in the larger concept of regional development in South Asia. The initial name of this procedure started in the 1940s when the First Asian Relations Conference was convened. It was the first effort to integrate the constructive forces in Asia into Anti-colonialism, World Peace, Anti-racialism problems and the necessity of economic development to complement political freedom. The approach continued into the 1980s with the establishment of the Colombo Powers Plan and the Bandung Afro-Asian Conference. Most of these efforts were mainly diplomatic.

1. Pandian, S.G. 2005. Energy Trade as a Confidence-building Measure between India and Pakistan: A Study of the Indo-Iran Trans-Pakistan Pipeline Project. Contemporary South Asia.

The second wave of the Asian process of regional integration reflects a pragmatic effort by the national governments of Asia to solve the specific challenges faced by the different areas of the continent. The emphasis moved from political problems to commercial relations. The significance of regional economic communities has grown quite important under the impact of this new thinking. The ASEAN Launched In 1967 and SAARC from a concept to a distributional reality in the 1980s provided flagrant instances. These organisations are widely involved in promoting economic, social and cultural integration. SAARC has intentionally avoided discussion of contentious issues relating to politics and security. It followed a progressive neo-functional strategy to wait until economic goals were achieved before dealing with political problems. The background and origin of SAARC nations will be in good shape.

1.3 Genesis of SAARC

Since the birth of nations worldwide and international organisations, the need for international Cooperation has been felt even a day before the establishment of the League of Nations; over time, several regional organisations, which were set up to ensure international Cooperation, have been created.

In Western Europe, the concept of regional economic Cooperation was initially devised to achieve the goal of socio-economic development, but in the developing world, where political choices were adopted at a premium, such a dominating role of the economic forces was not acceptable. Against the background, the earliest regional cooperation groups, including developing nations, have set security goals, not socio-economic development.

It must be said that, following the conclusion of the Second World War, the international situation changed at sea. Now, alliances were made sin-qua-non-after the cold war to broaden the sphere of influence. It was recognised that regional agricultural groups might fulfil the politico-strategic objectives of the industrialised world.[1]. Various organisations have come into existence in favour of the Western world, including the R.I.O. Pact, American states' organisations in Latin America, NATO in Western Europe, CENTO in West Asia, Association for South East Asia and subsequently

1. Plummer, M.G. 2006a. Toward Win-Win Regionalism in Asia: Issues and challenges in Forming Efficient Trade Agreements. Asian Development Bank Working Paper Series on Regional Economic Integration No. 5.

SEATO etc. These groups were primarily aimed at limiting the influence of the Soviet Union. In response to the West's regional organisations, the Soviet Union backed the creation of its Eastern European allies' regional organisations, such as the Warsaw Pact. The fundamental aim of forming these institutions was to safeguard the interests of the Member States.

In other areas of the third world, the concept of growth via regional Cooperation progressively becomes monetary. The newly independent nations of Asia and Africa have also embraced the notion that regional organisations may achieve their socio-economic growth. Various regional organisations, such as the Interamerican Development Bank, the Latin American Free Trade Association, the Arab League and the African States Organization etc., have been formed.

The non-aligned movement, popular among third-world nations, has given a basis for the Member States to take meaningful measures towards regional Cooperation. This movement had a significant influence on the establishment of O.A.U. and ASEAN. In addition, the creation of 77 was also carried out by N.A.M. in the United Nations.

It must be noted here that the idea of the region is developed from regionalism and regional Cooperation. An area must have similar geographical, economic, social, cultural and political features, etc. However, the South Asian region is an area of disparity and similarity. Our nation has a dominating position in the whole area. Other regions - Pakistan, Bangladesh, Bhutan, Nepal, Sri Lanka, and the Maldives may be referred to be peripheral nations from a geographical point of view. Another noteworthy geographic characteristic is that, except for India, no country in the area has a common boundary with the other. There are land borders with India in Pakistan, Nepal, Bhutan and Bangladesh, while Sri Lanka and the Maldives have maritime boundaries. Because of this unique geographical position, every nation in the area is intimately connected to India. In addition, India is dominating in the area for many reasons. It is 72a of the region's total area, 77a of the people, and 85a of the grown land. It also has the majority of the accessible natural resources in the area. In contrast with other nations in the region, it is considerably more developed. Because of these reasons, the smaller countries of South Asia have acquired a psychosis of dread towards India.

South Asian economies are not complementary either. On the other side, they are competitive. The political systems, philosophies, political connections, foreign policy direction and strategic unification of the nations of South Asia were likewise varied. However, there are more shared elements that link the countries of South Asia to a common heritage of the British empire. British imperialism has given rise to establishing similar political, administrative and juridical institutions in these nations. All countries in the area share similar ethnicity, language, religions, etc. In addition, their social structure, living style, faith system, and Tess are the same. It is a state fact that South Asia's future as a region relies on how they strongly use these shared characteristics to consolidate its regional identity.[1]

The history of regional cooperation efforts in South Asia may be split into two phases: pre-and post-1970. In the early stages, attempts to achieve regional Cooperation in South Asia were part of the Asian identity phenomena. Most Asian nations believed that they had comparable experiences of colonial exploitation and growth. They had to fight to safeguard their independence and sovereignty, and they would only solve these issues through mutual collaboration. Even before its independence, the Indian government was conscious of establishing Cooperation with South Asian countries. This was the subject of a resolution adopted by the Indian National Congress in 1928. Nehru believed that nations with comparable development difficulties and fighting for their freedom should work together to assist each other. In 1945 he said: "I stand for the Indian, Iranian, Iraqi, Afghan and Burmese South Asian Federations." Nehru convened the inaugural Asian Conference for Relations in New Delhi in 1947. It emphasised collaboration amongst the Asian nations. These conferences were held from 1947 to 1955 to identify the potential for Asian Cooperation. Other South Asian countries have also shown an interest in this area, with Sri Lanka proposing a permanent regional cooperation organisational framework. The 1955 Bandung Conference took a significant step towards collaboration on the Asian and African continents. Regional economic and intra-regional cooperation proposals have been made throughout Asia and Africa, but none could materialise.

These previous attempts in Asia and Southern Asia, in particular, have not yielded the expected outcomes for several reasons. The primary reasons for this failure were the inter-state conflicts, tensions, mistrust and apprehensions amongst the several nations.

1. Sobhan, R. 2008. Bangladeshi Perspectives on South Asian Regional Integration. Paper presented at the conference on "Does South Asia Exist? Prospects for Regionalism in South Asia". Stanford University.

New attempts to forge collaboration in South Asia started in the early 1970s. Ms Indira Gandhi sought to foster the spirit of regional Cooperation during her tour to Burma, Afghanistan and Indonesia. The various changes in South Asia throughout the early and late 1970s helped create a cosy environment for collaboration among Asian nations. The emergence of Bangladesh as an independent nation and the Indo-Soviet Treaty of 1971 gave India the dominant position. While India has successfully created cordial ties with Sri Lanka and Nepal, smaller countries have seen the merger of Sikkim into the Indian Union as proof of Indian hegemonic ambitions in the area.

The creation of new political regimes after 1976 in South Asia was a significant event in this area. All these governments need stability and political legitimacy, and thus they seek assistance from each other. In India, Janata's government took a gentle approach to neighbouring nations. In addition, the growing economic crisis, rising poverty, unemployment and decreasing growth rate had produced a cosy environment to attempt regional Cooperation.

Nepal, Sri Lanka and Bangladesh are the smallest nations in the area. In this respect, a specific proposal for regional Cooperation in South Asia came from the President of Bangladesh in May 1980. In reality, he had worked on this concept for a long time and asked India and other nations for their assistance. It was logical that the collaboration proposal amongst the area's countries originated from a smaller country to achieve two anticipated goals. It would conceal the hegemonic designs of India and speed up the region's economic growth. India welcomed the idea in principle but decided to examine it attentively before starting on the final choice. Pakistan believed that this plan would open the way for further strengthening India.

The idea of regional Cooperation was fictionalised in December 1985 after several meetings and deliberations among the constituent states.

Everyone would recognise that South Asia was exceptionally late in understanding the advantages of the regional cooperation system between all the well-defined areas. However, efforts in that respect led to the intended outcome in 1985. As was previously mentioned, the actual start was made by the Late Zia-ur-Rahman, President of Bangladesh. It was preceded by a preliminary study of President Rehman's proposal to the leaders of India and Pakistan in 1977, his travel to Sn" Lanka in 1979 and his visit to Bangladesh by King Birendra of Nepal in 1978. In May 1980, encouraged by his exchange of views with the leaders of those countries on the proposal, he wrote to the leaders of the States in the region, stressing the seriousness of a regional forum, indicating the fields of economic, technical, scientific, education, social and cultural Cooperation as possible." And he proposed a summit conference to achieve the goal.

Although all the nations in the area did not agree with President Rehman's plan, India and Pakistan were not enthused. Both rejected the idea of a summit conference and arranged for a ministerial meeting to be organised by tower-level officials. A conference at the summit level should only follow after the lesser level meetings have produced desired outcomes and the right and substantial basis for their success has been discussed."

While India's objection was due to the fear that its little neighbours could use the forum, in the long run, to pressure India collectively in bilateral matters and hamper its vital domestic interests, Pakistan's disinclination was the result of suspicion that this proposal could ultimately ensure the dominance of India over the region in general, and Pakistan in particulate matter. Pakistan likewise favoured the need to resolve the existing bilateral issues between the nations.[1]. In this case, Dawn (Karachi) pointed out that 'the lack of bilateral disputes and the presence of a shared sense of political end are two substantial grounds for a regional cooperation effort. Pakistan has also been cautious of its extensive participation in the South Asian area because its attempts to establish relations with the Islamic nations of West Asia may throw questions on its trustworthiness and sinuousness.

Diplomacy and discussions among foreign ministers of South Asian countries cleared misunderstandings regarding the plan during their trips to the United Nations from June to September 1980. The proposal's draught has been significantly modified. A consensus has developed in South Asia to construct regional Cooperation from underneath, avoiding disputes and collaboration, only in areas mutually advantageous to all seven countries in the region and in which there is no controversy."

Shortly after, the regional cooperation proposal was approved by the Member States at the official level, and on 25 November 1980, it was published and circulated. The article made a fretful appeal for an environment of trust and trust. Explaining the need to use the area's

1. Taneja, N. and A. Sawhney. 2007. Revitalising SAARC Trade: India's Role at 2007 Summit. Economic and Political Weekly. XLII (13). pp. 1081-1084.

resources, it reads: 'countries of the region, both bilaterally and regionally, collaborated under cover of forums such as the ESCAP, the Non-Aligned Movement and the Common Wealth. These initiatives have not thoroughly utilised the enormous potential or regional Cooperation available and the resultant advantage that this brings to the area's nations collectively and individually.

The report discussed unequal development levels in the area and proposed methods of rectifying them. It also highlighted eleven particular areas for starting the collaboration process. These included telecommunication, weather and transport, shipping, tourism, research in agriculture, joint ventures, development of the market, scientific and technological collaboration, and educational and cultural Cooperation.

The seven South Asian states' foreign secretaries officially met in Colombo in 1981 after the Dhaka proposal.

In the remarks of foreign ministers of seven States, there was a firm agreement on the necessity to strengthen Cooperation among them. While emphasising the shared historical geography, culture and tradition of the Subcontinent, the Sri Lankan delegate indicated the desire of successive Host Country governments for an integrated regional approach to their everyday challenges and ambitions.[1].

Both India and Pakistan, at this point, resisted the creation of any institution. As Riyaz Peiacha, Pakistan's Foreign Secretary, has said, let us tie the brick-by-brick cooperation structure and a strong and safe basis for that alone. The Indian Foreign Secretary emphasised two fundamental principles:

1. Unanimity decisions must be made.
2. The exclusion of contentious political topics.

All participants decided to move constantly and follow the concept of movement step by step. The idea of unanimity was also adopted, allowing all members the power to veto, and it was also decided that bilateral and controversial issues should not be discussed.

---

1. Udagedera, S. 2001. SAPTA Negotiations: Constraints and Challenges. In Impediments to Regional Economic Cooperation in South Asia, edited, Institute of Policy Studies of Sri Lanka and Coalition for Action on South Asian Cooperation in Association with Friederich-Ebert-Stiftung, Colombo Office.

The foreign secretaries established five research groups and designated a coordinator for each group. The selected coordinating nations in the agricultural, rural development, telecommunications, meteorology, and health and population sectors were Bangladesh, Sri Lanka, Pakistan, India and Nepal. An entire committee of semi or officers from seven nations, with Sri Lanka as coordinator, has been established to explore and report on additional possible areas of collaboration.

In November 1981, the second conference of foreign secretaries took place in Kathmandu. The joint communication emphasised establishing three research groups in transportation, postal services and scientific and technology companies. These groups were to be coordinated respectively by Maldives, Bhutan and Pakistan. It was also suggested that the five study groups recommended during the Colombo meetings should be converted into working groups with rotating chairs. Each group's job was to draw both immediate and long-term strategies. The primary action programme included data and information sharing, expert interchange, training facilities, and regional seminars and workshops. On the other hand, the long-term programme needed to incorporate the evaluation of needs and resources, the development of particular regional projects and mechanisms for project funding.

In August 1982, the third conference of foreign secretaries took place in Islamabad. The conference approved the suggestions of the five working groups and transformed the Kathmandu study groups into the working groups. Two additional research groups were established in sports and culture and in planning and development.

On the basis of reports by work groups, the Committee as a whole was asked to prepare an integrated action programme in the agreed cooperation areas and to recommend modalities and mechanisms for implementation, coordination and monitoring of the agreed action programme, and to provide, where possible, indications of financial implications of t's short-term component.

In Dhaka in March 1983 the fourth-round conference of the foreign secretaries took place. Foreign Secretaries agreed immediately on the necessary ways to start regional Cooperation. Foreign Ministers approved the I.P.A. (Integrated Program of Action) and agreed to officially launch it at the ministerial conference in Delhi in July 1983, followed by the meeting of foreign secretaries.

The Seven South Asian State Foreign Ministers met in New Delhi in August 1983. The Regional Cooperation of South Asia was formally launched, and the Joint Declaration signed that regional Cooperation of the type envisaged in the action plan is not a substitute for the bilateral and multilateral commitments and will not impede Member States from joining other international forms[1].

As regards institutional structures, it was agreed to establish technical committees. A Technical Committee accessible to all the forum nations was responsible for implementing, co-coordinating and monitoring the programmes, with the following terms of reference, in every field of Cooperation: a) Determining regional cooperation potential and scope in agreed areas, b) formulating action programmes and drafting projects c) determining the financial implications of sector-based programmes of action d) Implementing and coordinating sector action programmes, and e) monitoring the progress made with implementation. In the event of initiatives involving more than two counties but not all countries of the area, 'the Action Committee composed of the countries concerned may, with the previous permission of this standing committee, be established up for execution. For coordinating and monitoring regional Cooperation and the activity of the technical committee, the standing committee should be set up at the level of foreign secretaries.

The Foreign Ministers of the forum met in July 1984 in Male for the first time then in May 1985 in Thimpu. In Male the idea was suggested to convene the ministerial conference in some of the vital areas of Cooperation that have previously been agreed on. In Thimpu, there developed an agreement on the idea of building up a formal organisation as the highest political entity with the Council of Ministers.

1.4 SAARC: Its significance for South Asia

SAARC was developed to satisfy the need to strengthen the inherent geographical, social, cultural and economic homogeneity achieved through some kind of institutionalisation among South Asian nations. It offers a faint, foggy, feasible platform for unification amid a sea of conflict and remarkable variety. The following reasons highlight the need for SAARC to solve the challenges facing the nations in the region:

1. Weerakoon, D. 2001. Impediments to Regional Economic Cooperation in South Asia, edited by Saman Kelegama. Institute of Policy Studies of Sri Lanka and Coalition for Action on South Asian Cooperation in Association with Friederich-Ebert Stiftung, Colombo Office.

The SAARC nations are the poorest in the world, and rapid population growth rates further undermine the pitiful economic position. The South Asian nations fall into the underlying class of the less developed third-world states in every conceivable development indicator, including health and nutrition, education, capital housing, transport and communication, and agriculture.

Expanding economic integration in the area is essential since the international and commercial environments have experienced a shift to the third-world deterrent. The decrease in assistance, the growing weight of debt servicing, worsening trade conditions, and the northern nations' propensity to erect unjustified hurdles against developing countries have been essential obstacles in third-world countries' journey.[1].

Given the tremendous benefits generated by the optimal exploitation of the regional natural resources of the area via integrated management and the sharing of experiences and technology in different development sectors, a cooperative approach is inevitable.

There is a wide range of regional Cooperation amongst SAARC nations since they share many shared consensuses and have many comparable issues. It goes without saying that regional Cooperation between these nations would result in fast economic growth and reinforce their mutual ties.

In its current stage of growth, SAARC is faced with many difficulties, regardless of the significant economic differences, which include the various political-security views of the Member States, their variety in their size and degree of development. It takes political determination and a genuine commitment from local leaders to overcome the dividing factors that dominate and solidify and harmonise a single front for mutually beneficial links in many areas of activity. When the cold war ends, global problems need a collaborative effort for all the major countries involved; regions and nations work together towards commons. The changing global environment demands total participation from all SAARC nations. Following this success, SAARC will play an essential role in moving the Member States and their people closer to achieving good international integration.

1. Asian Development Bank. 2007. South Asia Economic Report, Foreign Direct Investment in South Asia. December. Manila.

SAARC's unique characteristics and its existing significant structures:

South Asia is a special area, and its history and its structural problems continue to be subject to some of the unique features of this area are listed below:

1. Indo-centric-region is South Asia. Three-quarters of India comprises over 70a of the entire regional area, three-fourths of its people and approximately two-thirds of its G.N.P. Almost all states are Indian neighbours, but none are neighbours. The ten-strong and dominant Indian strategies create anxiety and conflict amongst other nations in the area. Finally, the quality of life is based on the term poor, from poor to very poor.
2. Unlike the E.E.C. and ASEAN, where there has been a significant external danger, the South Asian nations have no shared threat perceptions and have not been driven to react in the same way that E.E.C. or ASEAN members did. Most of these nations believe that the danger comes from internal or regional problems. Against this background, SAARC has chosen not to emphasise the resolution of disputes but has resolved to promote regional, positive socio-economic Cooperation[1].
3. The third distinctive feature is the absence of SAARC as opposed to many regional organisations, owing to the efforts of the region's major nations. In fact, via the combined efforts of the smaller countries, it saw the light of day. It was initiated by the late President of Bangladesh, Zia-ur-Rahman. It took two years to institutionalise the concept of a regional South Asian organisation. The previous Bangladeshi President reorganised the cultural and ethical communities and toured most of the South Asian capital to develop leaders' thoughts on creating a regional organisation.
4. SAARC was formed due to local initiatives and efforts, and no external agency was directly or indirectly engaged. Despite complicated disputes in the area, cooperative enterprises in South Asia quickly gained momentum. The necessity for Cooperation in the several non-political spheres was recognised, which in turn gave rise to SAARC.

---

1. Yeats, A. J. 1997. Does Mercosur's Trade Performance Raise Concerns about the Effects of Regional Trade Arrangements? World Bank Policy Research Working Paper No. 1729.

5. Another distinctive feature of the SAARC is its concentration on socio-economic development alone. This is the one characteristic which distinguishes it from the rest. This focus must be considered, given the continuous and complicated conflicts which have often led to significant wars and revolutions in the area. The game's name was the mutual hostility and use of the problems of others for both the Indians and Pakistanis. Both states did not miss the chance to make life hard for the other. However, one finds that the regional nations likewise believed that a regional organisation has to be created.

SAARC is the result of attempts to encourage not just cement connections among the South Asian States in different sectors, such as diplomatic, social and economic affairs, but also collective autonomy and to enhance South Asian quality of life. To achieve these goals, the SAARC nations agreed to set up a regional cooperative organisation and quickly agreed that a collaborative strategy would be used step by step. In less than ten years, SAARC has been able to identify several areas of cooperative Cooperation, including agriculture, forestry, health, population, meteorology, rural development, transport and science, postal services and technology, postal service, sport, arts, culture, drug trafficking and tourism development, and so on.[1]. Of course, most of these sectors belong in the outermost regions. Still, a triumphant cooperative march in these areas was anticipated to encourage the members to develop the core areas of Cooperation further. However, development here is hindered not only by the Member States' diverse views but also by clear political and economic restrictions.

1.5 Evolution of SAARC

Under Article 52 of the Charter of the United Nations, the South Asian Association for Regional Cooperation (SAARC) established regional agreements or institutions for the management of international peace and security, with the aim and principles of the United Nations Charter

It was founded after four and a half years of preparation on 8 December 1985. The Association's fundamental goal is to expedite the process of economic and social development in the Member States via combined action in the specified areas of Cooperation. In the South Himalayas, the

1. World Bank. 2004. Trade Policies in South Asia: An Overview. Washington, D.C.

SAARC area is bordered by Hindu Kush Mountains. Late President Zia-Ur-Rehman of the Republic of Bangladesh, who toured Nepal, India, Pakistan and Sri Lanka during 1977-78, began the concept of regional collaboration in South Asia to investigate regional economic Cooperation among SAARC countries. He advocated collective self-reliance in all these nations' shared search for peace and prosperity.[1]. A formal appeal for SAARC Regional Cooperation was made in May 1980. His call was answered positively by all SAARC nations. Consequently, discussions were conducted at the official level for the planned collaboration. These preliminary exchanges have clearly shown that regional Cooperation, in turn, should reflect a spirit of mutual trust, and an awareness of the political inspiration existing among the countries of the region and such Cooperation should be based on equal sovereignty, territorial integrity and non-interference in

Foreign secretaries of seven nations initially met in Colombo (Sri Lanka) for regional Cooperation in April 1981, namely Bangladesh, Bhutan, India, the Maldives, Nepal, Pakistan and Sri Lanka. Regional Cooperation was decided that the national ambitions of the SAARC nations should be founded on mutual trust, understanding and sympathy. Five major sectors, including agriculture, rural development, telecommunications, meteorology, and health and demographic activities, have been identified here.

India has always been actively interested in and strongly dedicated to regional Cooperation in order to resolve shared issues in many areas, such as cultural and economic policy. Jawaharlal Nehru, India's great leader and prime minister, stressed in his speeches and in writing frequently the unity and solidarity of Asia. In his maiden broadcast to the country on 7 September, 1946, Jawaharlal Nehru stated, "We are from Asia and the people of Asia are closer and closer to us. India is thus positioned that it is the focal point of West, Southeast and Southeast Asia." Similarly, Nehru repeated the same occasion: "When talking about Asia, remember that India has to play a very significant role in Asia, not because of its ambitions but because of the force of the circumstances, because of geography, because of history and many other reasons... You have to stay in contact with the other areas, even if you think in terms of regional organisations in Asia. And no matter whatever areas you consider, India's significance cannot be disregarded.

1. Ali, E. & Talukder D.K. (2009). "Preferential trade among the SAARC countries. Prospects and challenges of regional integration in South Asia", JOAAG, Vol. 4. no. 1

In addition, Nehru stressed that the nations of Asia must meet equally in a shared mission with Endeavor in order to maintain an environment of cordiality and collaboration at the Asian Relations Conference in New Delhi. He stated "It is appropriate for India to do its role in this new era of Asian development." Nehru was convinced and hoped that some permanent Asian Institute would be a school of Asian studies to investigate shared issues and establish closer relationships.

"I will not list all the topics, since it is up to you to debate and decide on them. The concept of regional Cooperation in South Asia was originally proposed in May 1980. The first meeting in Colombo in April 1981 followed by foreign secretaries from seven nations, namely India, Pakistan, Bhutan, Bangladesh, Nepal, Sri Lanka and the Maldives. Regional Cooperation was formally formed on 8 December 1985.

Membership of SAARC includes Bangladesh, Bhutan, India, Maldives, Nepal, Sri Lanka and Pakistan. Afghanistan is the eighth SAARC member. The area is vital for military, commerce, transport population expansion, and economic development in India directly and indirectly between East and West. In defence, commerce and maritime transport, the Indian Ocean plays a key role in the nearby majority of nations in South Asia.

The SAARC area accounts for 3.3% of the globe and a fifth of its people. All SAARC nations may be divided into categories. Firstly, Bhutan and Nepal are two landlocked nations. Secondly, two islands are present, such as Sri Lanka and Maldives and third, India, Pakistan and Bangladesh, with the South- and South-West Indian Ocean and the Indo-Gangetic Plains extending along these nations.

Most people in SAARC nations rely on farming and are poorly educated, lack science and technology, and are overpopulated. Most nations rely on assistance and trade from the industrialised countries.

On 8 December 1985 the South Asian Regional Cooperation Association was established as the first step towards a regional company. A decade after SAARC was formed, at the end of the year the South Asian Free Preferential Trading Agreement (SAPTA) was introduced. 2001 was set a deadline for the South Asian Free Trade Association to conclude a pact (SAFTA). The SAARC has signed a Treaty which will lead in future to free trade and the movement of products which would pave the way for the South Asian Economic Union in the direction of the E.U.[1].

1. Isher judge Ahluwalia. (2013). "Economic cooperation in south Asia". Indian council for research on international economic relations.

The Treaty of South Asia's Free Trade Association (SAFTA) aims at removing trade obstacles, phasing out tariffs and creating a ministerial tariff management system and settling disputes among its members. This Treaty was due to be concluded by 1 January 2006. Indeed, the exchange of nations with mutual experience is more relevant, more economical and cheaper and gives a wide range of opportunities for mutual collaboration in different fields. For many years to come, agriculture will continue to dominate their economies. The primary market products are the economic development such as food for the increasing population, feed for animals, raw materials and the market for industry.

Principles

- Cooperation within the framework of the Association is based on respect for the principles of sovereign equality, territorial integrity, political independence, non-interference in the internal affairs of other states and mutual benefit.
- Such Cooperation is to complement and not to substitute bilateral or multilateral Cooperation. Such Cooperation should be consistent with bilateral and multilateral obligations of the member states.
- Decisions at all levels in SAARC are taken on the basis of unanimity.
- Bilateral and contentious issues are excluded from its deliberations.

1.6 Profile of the SAARC Member States

South Asia extends south from the central part of the continent to the Indian Ocean. The main borders of South Asia are the Indian Ocean, the Himalayas and Afghanistan. The Arabian Sea borders Pakistan and India to the West, and the Bay of Bengal borders India and Bangladesh to the east. The Western Frontier is a desert region where Pakistan shares a border with Iran.

South Asian countries include Sri Lanka, India, Bangladesh, Bhutan, Nepal, Pakistan and the Maldives. The Himalayas, separating South Asia from East Asia along the border of China's Tibet Autonomous Region, are the world's highest mountains and the dominant physical feature of the northern edge of South Asia. Other countries that share the Himalayas include Nepal, Bhutan, India and Pakistan. Further north along the

Himalayan mountain range, the traditional region of Kashmir is divided between India, Pakistan and China. On the opposite side of the Himalayas are two island countries off the coast of South India. The first is Sri Lanka, a large tropical island off the southeast coast of India, and the second is the Republic of Maldives, an archipelago (group of islands) off the southwest coast of India. The Maldives comprises nearly 1,200 islands barely rising above sea level; the highest elevation is just seven feet, seven inches. Only about two hundred islands are inhabited in the Maldives.

Balancing natural capital and population growth will remain a primary concern in the empire's future. South Asia is very populous, with approximately one and a half billion people representing various ethnic and cultural groups. The diverse population was amalgamated into political units rooted in the empire's colonial past, primarily in Great Britain. British colonialism significantly impacted the area; its long-term effects include political division and conflict in places like Kashmir and Sri Lanka.[1]

There is perhaps no other historical example like South Asia of a geographically and historically contiguous region with widely shared social, cultural, linguistic and spiritual practices experiencing a continuous fragmentation of its once reasonably integrated economic space. South Asia has the dubious distinction of having an even more significant number of poor people living below $1 per day than sub-Saharan Africa. Border regions where central policy-making in any country is peripheral and where this poverty is primarily concentrated will benefit significantly from greater regional economic cooperation because it opens up these borders and converts peripheries to new poles of economic activity.[2]. Historically, the best example is the development of Northern Italy and Southern Switzerland. More significant cross-border flows became possible with the Mont Blanc tunnel opening under the Alps, drastically reducing travel times and space up the border regions on both sides. A similar growth-generating impact can be expected in the Eastern areas of South Asia, where Bangladesh, Bhutan, India and Nepal are close to each other through greater regional cooperation. This would make existing national borders, which arbitrarily divided organically integrated communities, again irrelevant.

1. South Asia: Retrieved September 23, 2022, from: https://saylordotorg.github.io/text_world-regional-geography-people-places-and-globalization/s12-south-asia.html
2. Bhan, Pankaj, Srivastava, R.N., SAARC – Evolutionary Cycle of Growth and Consolidation, in SAARC Socio-Economic Transformation Foundation for peace and sustainable development, (Delhi: D.K. Fine Art Press Pvt. Ltd, 2008)

India has urged the member states to put aside their rivalries and concentrate their attention and energies on regional development delivering win-win results. Despite this, the hostility between the two developed regional powers- India and Pakistan- as well as the in-built asymmetry in the Indo-centric region and the consequent threat perception among smaller countries of the region, has frustrated India's sincere but cautious attempts to make SAARC a meaningful and productive regional organisation.

1.6.1 India

India is the world's second most populous country (after China) and the seventh largest in area. With a land area of 32 87 263 sq. km, India is about 3,000 km (1,875 miles) long and 3,000 km wide and has, because of its peninsular shape, a shoreline of about 7,000 km(4,400 miles) along the Bay of Bengal on the east and the Arabian Sea on the West. The land frontier of about 5,700 km (3,600 miles) is shared with Pakistan on the West- by China (mainly Tibet), Nepal and Bhutan on the north, and by Bangladesh and Myanmar (Burma) on the east. The Indian Island groups of Lakshadweep are off the western coast, and the Andaman and Nicobar Islands are located in the eastern part of the Bay of Bengal. India has a rich and varied minerals-resource base. Coal and iron ore are abundant and located close to each other in the Chota Nagpur Plateau in the eastern peninsula. Manganese, lignite, copper bauxite, kyanite, fire clays, mica, and limestones are in large quantities.[1].

India's Initiatives Towards Regional Cooperation

Pre-independence initiatives: The idea of transnational/regional/ Asian identity in search for a meaningful role in international affairs has been an essential ingredient of the Indian mindset during the struggle for independence from the British Empire fact, the Indian National Congress kept its focus on India's possible role in Asia during the freedom struggle. It was as early as 1920 that Gandhiji wrote of the growing solidarity of the Asian countries. In 1922, C.R. Das, President of the Indian National Congress, urged India's participation in an Asian Federation, which he regarded as inevitable. Congress adopted a resolution to this effect in 1928. In 1945 Pt. Jawaharlal Nehru declared that the small states of the world would have no future and that they were sure to be reduced to the status of satellite states; therefore, he advocated the creation of the South Asian

1. Chaudhary, Anasua Basu Ray, SAARC at Cross Roads, The Fate of Regional Cooperation in South Asia, (New Delhi: Shivam Offset Press, 200)

Federation of India, Iran, Iraq, Afghanistan and Burma. Even before India's formal independence from British rule, the leaders of the Indian National Movement convened an Asian Relations Conference.

Asian Relations Conference (ARC): On the eve of Indian independence inspired by Nehru, the Indian Council of World Affairs (ICWA) convened an Asian Relations Conference (ARC) in New Delhi in March 1947. The Conference was attended by 28 countries, including the then-Soviet Asian Republics and Egypt. There were observers from the UNO, Arab League and several institutions from Sydney, London, Moscow and New York. Eight different subjects by five groups were discussed at the Conference. These were as follows:

- National movements for freedom
- Racial problems and Inter-Asian Migrations
- The transition from colonial to National Economy; Agricultural Reconstruction and Industrial Development; Labour Problems and Social services;
- Cultural problems
- Status of women and women's movement.

However, there was distrust among the small Asian Countries towards their powerful neighbours despite this general agreement. An attempt was made to create an Asian Relations Organization (ARO), which continued as a non-official organisation for about a decade before being wound up in 1957.

Jawaharlal Nehru was the President of the provisional General Council of the ARO. But the distrust, suspicion and rivalry of Asian nations must have come as a rude shock to the intellectual idealism and honesty of purpose of Jawaharlal Nehru. "Faced with the hostility of Arabs, India had no bricks to build any Asian structure."[1].

India's approach in ARC was that the Conference was not directed against any race or region, that it ought not to deal with bilateral internal disputes and that there were no leaders and no followers among the participants. This approach was to continue in future in all Afro-Asian Conferences held during the decade and a half after Indian independence, viz., the New Delhi Conference on Indonesia (1949), the Baguio (Philippines)

1. Emanual Nahar, Sheveta Sehgal, SAARC in Contemporary World: Issues and Concerns, New Delhi, Swastik Publications, 2014.

conference (May 1950), the Colombo powers Conference (April 1954), the Bogor Conference (Dec. 1954), the Afro-Asian Conference (April 1954), the Brioni Conference, July 1956 and the Belgrade Conference, 1961. Dutch police action in Indonesia in December 1948. The Conference was attended by India, Afghanistan, Australia, Burma, Ceylon, Egypt, Ethiopia, Iran, Iraq, Lebanon, Pakistan, the Philippines, Saudi Arabia and Yemen, and observers from Kumitang, China, Nepal, New Zealand, and Thailand condemned the Dutch aggression and called for the realisation of the arrested members of the Government of the Indonesia Republic, withdrawal of Dutch troops from the capital Jog Jakarta and from Indonesia at large to transfer power by January 1, 1950, to the United States of Indonesia.

The objective of the Conference was to discuss the Indonesian struggle for freedom. This Conference, unlike earlier ones, was official in character and political in nature. Jawaharlal Nehru, the then prime Minister of India, while strongly criticising the Dutch action against Indonesia, also made an emotional appeal for more significant interaction among Asian Countries. But he was charged by The New York Times for the growth of regionalism and racialism. Soviet newspaper Pravada also attacked Nehru for being anti-Soviet and interpreted the Asian Conference on Indonesia as an attempt to establish an anti-Soviet bloc.

India's approach to regional cooperation took a different turn when the United States agreed to give military aid to Pakistan in 1954, thus upsetting the entire balance of power in the region and bringing the superpower rivalry to the doorsteps of South Asia. Nehru strongly criticised the formation of military pacts like SEATO and the Baghdad Pact. However, the attempts for regional cooperation continued at various levels, and the Bandung conference is regarded as the highest point of a shot.

India as Summit Chairman: Outcome

At the Bangalore Summit, held from lóto November 17, 1986, Heads of State and Government approved the following ideas aimed at strengthening cooperative programmes under SAARC:

- A South Asian Broadcasting Programme was covering both radio and television.
- Concrete steps should be taken to facilitate tourism in the region, including facilities for limited convertibility of national currencies for tourists from SAARC countries.

- Creation of the SAARC Documentation Centre as the repository of reliable and up-to-date information about technical, scientific and development matters.
- A concerted programme of exchange of scholars should be formulated, and action should be taken for an early institution of SAARC scholarships, fellowships and chairs to promote greater cross-fertilisation of ideas through more significant interaction among scholars, students and academics in the South Asian countries.

1.6.2 Bangladesh

Bangladesh emerged as an independent country on December 16 1971. Its official name is the "People's Republic of Bangladesh". Dhaka is the capital of Bangladesh and Bangle is the state language. The Independence and National Day of Bangladesh are on March 26. The population of the country stands at 123.15 million (2001). About 80 per cent of the people live in rural areas, and sixty per cent depend on agriculture for their livelihood. The four major religions in the country are Islam, Hinduism, Buddhism and Christianity.[1]. Muslims represent roughly 88 per cent of the population and Hindus about 10 per cent. The Constitution provides religious and cultural freedom to all inhabitants of Bangladesh. Bangladesh is a unitary, independent, sovereign republic with three essential organs: the Executive, the Legislature, and the Judiciary. The President is the Head of State and is chosen by the members of Parliament. The President acts in line with the Prime Minister's recommendation to the Executive Head. Bangladesh is predominantly an agricultural economy. Agriculture is the single most significant industry in the economy, contributing roughly 30 per cent of the country's GDP and employing about 60 per cent of the entire workforce. The nation has many big, medium and small-sized enterprises in both the public and private sectors based on indigenous and imported raw resources. Among these are jute, cotton, textiles, fertiliser, engineering, shipbuilding, steel, oil refinery, paper, newspaper, sugar, chemicals, cement and leather. The total Exports and Imports of Bangladesh in 2000 were U.S. $5590 Million and the U.S. $8993 Million correspondingly, of which 11.68 percent of imports and 1.57 per cent of exports are from SAARC nations.

1. Dhar, B., P. De, G. Das, and B. Singh, 2011. Expansion of North East India's Trade and Investment with Bangladesh and Myanmar: An Assessment of the Opportunities and Constraints. Research and Information System for Developing Countries (RIS), Ministry of Development of North Eastern Region and North Eastern Council.

Bangladesh's Position regarding Transit with Regional Countries

The topic of connectivity encompasses all modes of cross-border transportation. In Bangladesh–India ties, the discussion of a vehicle has picked up steam. The main problem is the transit of products from West to northeast India across Bangladesh territory. On the other hand, Bangladesh would welcome India's opening up Nepal and Bhutan to its trade. Nepal and Bhutan want to use India's road and rail networks to reach Bangladeshi ports for international commerce. Roads, rivers, trains, and any combination of these are all viable modes of transportation. India has set up transit facilities along its borders to facilitate trade with Nepal and Bhutan. As a result, these nations can do business with Bangladesh by rail and road and export and import commodities to and from other countries via Bangladesh. The Bangladesh–India connection negotiations have progressed since the joint communiqué in 2010 but have halted for various reasons. Service charges and user fees for public transportation facilities need to be addressed. Bangladesh has identified several possible transport routes based on distance, duration, and cost. Bulk items can be transported more cheaply by water or rail, but high-value commodities may be transported more efficiently by road. Routes that might be placed into service as quickly as feasible have been identified in this aspect.

It's widely agreed upon that a well-executed transit arrangement might be mutually beneficial for both nations. The nations must agree on service charges and user fees for transit facilities to pay the infrastructure's long-term expenses. This won't be easy. Because Bangladesh's present transportation infrastructure cannot handle the extra traffic expected from any conceivable transit arrangement with India, improving the routes would need considerable investment. The development of transit-related infrastructure in Bangladesh requires a thorough action plan that includes resources necessary for enhancing current infrastructure and regular maintenance.

1.6.3 Bhutan

People in Bhutan name their nation Druk-Yul, the land of Druks (the people) and Druks (the land). There is just one official language in Bhutan, and that is Dzongkha. Ancient records of the kingdom's past remain a secret. It is apparent, however, that Buddhism has played a significant role in moulding Bhutan's history from the 8th century A.D. In the 17th century, Bhutan was united under central rule and had remained so ever since. The current population of Bhutan is 638,000 people. The Druklpas, who are Buddhists, and the Lhotsampas, or southerners, who are mostly Hindus of Nepali descent, make up the majority of Bhutanese citizens.[1]. Ugyen Wangchuck formed the Wangchuck dynasty in 1907, which is still in charge of the country today. For decades, Bhutan's kings have been the driving force behind sweeping reforms in the country's legislative, judicial and administrative structures. A new Council of Ministers chosen by the National Assembly was given complete executive authority by the current monarch, King Jigme Singye Wangchuck, as part of a power transfer in 1998. Subsistence farming is the primary income source for most Bhutanese citizens. With hydroelectric power production and sales now accounting for over 30% of GDP, agriculture's proportion of the country's total output has fallen to less than 50%. 30,000 MW of electricity may be generated from the country's rivers. Bhutan also exports calcium carbide, timber products, and cement in addition to power. Known as Gross National Happiness (GNH), Bhutan's development ideology is drawing attention from all across the globe. It prioritises sound government, the advancement of culture, the protection of the environment, and the economy's growth.

Despite being a tiny landlocked nation in South Asia, Bhutan has consistently maintained peace within and beyond the Shangrila. Consistent with its neighbours, Bhutan is landlocked and crucial in terms of its position, making it an attractive target for terrorist groups. Consequently, it has faced several threats in the past. Despite this, Bhutan has made steady progress toward modernity and democracy over the last several decades.[2]. As the world's youngest democracy, Bhutan's transition to democracy in 2008 was accompanied by calm and unanimity, which was a cause for celebration. Initially, Bhutan's foreign policy was based on self-isolation; nevertheless, the country has never hesitated to adapt to changes in the global environment, which can be seen in its engagement and collaboration in South Asian and global concerns.

A national policy is a collection of rules and regulations that govern the activities of a country. The primary purpose of any country's national policy is to preserve the national interest. As well as internal events, relationships with foreign nations play an important role in maintaining

1. Saklani, Udisha & Tortajada, Cecilia.(2019), India's Development Cooperation In Bhutan's Hydropower Sector: Concerns And Public Perception, Water Alternatives,12(2).
2. Muni, S.D.(1984), Bhutan Steps Out, The World Today, 40(12).

a country's national interest. Foreign policies are determined by each nation, taking into account their strengths and limitations and changing social, economic, political, and strategic considerations. All states must have a distinct foreign policy for international politics to work. For various reasons, foreign policy refers to a country's approach to international relations. Foreign relations include a wide variety of topics, including politics, military, culture, economics, and technology.[1].

It is impossible for a country to ignore international politics in an era of liberalisation, privatisation, globalisation, and the internet. In today's world, it is impossible for a nation to remain disconnected from the rest of the globe. In a world of interconnection, no nation can be self-sufficient. Because of this, all nations now recognise the need to maintain good connections with other countries to further their growth. In developing its foreign policy, every country considers how to best advance its national and international interests while safeguarding its territorial integrity and sovereignty. This is particularly true for nations that aren't large. All countries have some foreign policy, but each country's principles, concepts, and strategies vary widely. Several elements are at play for a country's foreign policy to be effective. The most essential aspect affecting a country's foreign policy is its geographic location. In determining a nation's self-sufficiency, geography plays a role. Climate, soil fertility, water bodies, and landlocked status are all considered part of geography.

An individual country's foreign policies are also influenced by the country's history, customs and culture. After the end of colonialism in 1947, India's foreign policy focused on supporting liberation movements across the globe, from Indonesia to Vietnam and beyond. Similarly, public opinion, the domestic environment, and the country's ideology all have a role in determining foreign policy, in naming a few. Different countries have different factors that influence foreign policy; therefore, it's impossible to have a country's politics without having some foreign policy. Each country's path in foreign policy growth and development is unique. Bhutan's foreign policy has followed and navigated a similar approach, one that has remained so vibrant throughout the years, with its distinct traditions and ideals.

1. Borah, Rupakjyoti (2018), Japanese Foreign Minister's Bhutan Visit: Enhancing the Bilateral Relationship, Institute of South Asian Studies, National University of Singapore.

1.6.4 The Maldives

The civilisations of the Maldives date back more than 2000 years. Archaeological findings from many ancient sites in the Maldives show ruins of old Buddhist structures, some dating back to the 3rd and 4th centuries. The evidence shows that at the time of conversion to Islam in 1153 A.D., the population of the Maldives was mainly Buddhist. The archipelago of the Republic of Maldives is made up of a chain of 1190 small and low-lying islands, stretching over 800 km from north to south. Out of them, only 198 islands are inhabited. The population of the Maldives is 270,101 (2000 census). Maldivians comprise a mixed race, unified through sharing a common history, language and religion. Dhivehi is the official language. Islam is the strength and backbone of the country, permeating the entire fabric of the Maldivian culture, polity and civil society. The Maldives' political system is a unique blend of its history, traditions, Islamic faith and modem democratic principle. It has evolved over many years, the first written Constitution having been proclaimed in 1932, though unwritten constitutional principles had existed long before then. A republican form of government in 1968 replaced the constitutional monarchy with an Executive President as the Head of State.

The country adopted a new Constitution that is more comprehensive and in tune with the country's democratic principles on January 1 1998. The mainstay of the Maldives economy today composes fisheries and tourism. Nearly 19% of the labour force is engaged in the fisheries sector, which accounts for over 6% of the GDP. Tourism, which became a major industry in the mid-eighties, accounts for 33% of the GDP. The industrial activity consists of a traditional and a modem sector. The traditional sector consists of boat building, mat-weaving, rope making, blacksmithing, handicrafts and other cottage industries. The activities in the modem sector include fish canning, manufacture of garments, construction of fiberglass boats, and production of cleaning fluids and bottling of aerated water.[1].

1.6.5 Pakistan

On August 14, 1947, the Islamic Republic of Pakistan was declared by Quaid-e-Azam (the Great Leader) Muhammad Ali Jinnah, who is considered Pakistan's founding father. There are four provinces in Pakistan: Sindh, Baluchistan, Punjab, and NWFP. Islamabad serves as the nation's

1. Rehman, S.(1999). Regional Economic Cooperation in South Asia. In Ghosh, P. K.(Ed.), A Modernisation Perspective(pp. 268- 271).London: Greenwood Press.

capital and is located northwest of the country. Pakistan has an area of 796,095 square kilometres. In 2002, the country's population was 145.96 million. Urdu is the national language, although English is the official language. Islam is Pakistan's dominant religion, accounting for 95% of the population. Besides Hinduism and Christianity, there are other tiny religious communities of Sikhs, Parsis, and Buddhists. The government of Pakistan is divided into three distinct branches, each headed by a president. The Lower House (National Assembly) and the Upper House make up the legislative body (Senate). The President, the Prime Minister, and the National Security Council make up the administration. About 46.1% of the workforce is employed in agriculture-related activities, which account for 25% of GDP. GDP is now growing at a 3.6% annual pace. Mechanical and electrical equipment, petroleum products, transportation equipment, metals and metal products are some of the most typical imports, as fertiliser and foodstuffs, which are very important. The country's primary exports are cotton textiles, cotton yarn and thread, clothes, raw cotton, rice, carpets and rugs, leather, sports items, handicraft, fish, and fruit. Among Pakistan's total exports and imports in 2000, 2.32 per cent came from SAARC nations and 2.92 per cent from the rest of the world, totalling $9,156 million and $11,049 million, respectively.

Unsettled boundaries (a legacy of colonial rule) and violent actions over cross-border occurrences have long been associated with conventional security risks and violent disputes among SAARC members. Terrorism and religious intolerance have both become severe security concerns. Indian Prime Minister Narendra Modi called the horrible assaults on a Pakistani school in December an assault on all of humankind. At the time of this writing, Prime Minister Modi has called on all Indian schools to observe two minutes of quiet protest at what he termed an "unthinkable act of barbarism" against Pakistan. Religious principles that have been politicised, perverted, and exploited pose a considerable danger to security in all SAARC nations.[1]. Gunrunning, drug trafficking, human smuggling, and piracy are just a few of the illegal activities now posing a danger to the security of South Asian countries, thanks to organised crime groups operating across the Indian Ocean. Threats to SAARC collaboration are increasingly being promoted. Anti-narcotics and psychotropic drug trafficking, weapons smuggling, money laundering, counterfeit currency, and other transnational crimes are

1. Sattar, A. (2010). Pakistan's Foreign Policy (1947-2009): A Concise History. Karachi: Oxford Unversity Press.

all addressed in the Kathmandu Declaration. SAARC has also agreed to set up a desk to monitor cybercrime.

Analysing SAARC's agenda from its start may help construct the balance sheet. The organisation's focus has shifted from social to economic and now includes national security. Additional protocols, drug trafficking, etc., are on the security agenda. Free trade regimes have also replaced preferential trade regimes, and it has been created with three windows: economic, social and infrastructural. In the future, there will be a discussion of a South Asia Economic Union and the creation of a SAARC bank.[1]. It is impossible to evaluate SAARC without acknowledging the challenges of bringing together nations that share distrust and suspicion and are still burdened by the legacy of separation.

As a result of a lack of coordination between regional and national priorities, SAARC development stalled. In addition, Pakistan has thwarted trade and connectivity measures that would have eased regional economic integration because of the India-Pakistan bilateral conflict. In the wake of this, bilateral efforts were born. However, regional multilateralism has not been entirely replaced by bilateralism. The area is moving toward deeper integration, but Pakistan's stance toward regional connectivity is proving to be a key roadblock. India would get a direct line to Afghanistan via connectivity, something Islamabad opposes.

Economic integration has been one of the most important areas of cooperation, which would ease commerce and link the nations. India has a crucial role because of its geography and foreign policy that aspires to integrate the area. The promise of economic benefits, such as job creation and greater economic activities linked to trade, is likely to lead to peace in any development endeavour.[2].

Insecurity, economic turmoil, and social difficulties are just a few of the concerns that the area is now dealing with. SAARC member states can work together to overcome these problems. Through cooperative efforts, the SAARC organisation may achieve its economic, cultural, and social development objectives, as well as a state of collective self-reliance. ASEAN member countries can settle both local and regional concerns, provided their leaders are genuine about this, and if there is confidence

1. Rehman, S. (2016, November 10). Second opinion-Foreign Policy in Crisis: Can Pakistan Overcome. Retrieved from Jinnah Institute: Jinnah institue.org
2. Ahmad, S., Kelegama, S., & Ghani, E. (2010). Promoting Economic Cooperation in South Asia: Beyond SAFTA. Retrieved from The World Bank: www.worldbank.org

among the member nations (Kaler, 2016). An active SAARC participant, Pakistan helps to foster regional collaboration and prosperity while also helping to maintain regional peace and security. Throughout all of the organisation's meetings, Pakistan has emphasised the need to maintain a safe and peaceful environment in South Asia in order to pursue joint interests in social well-being, economic growth, and prosperity. According to Pakistan, a significant boost to the organisation would come from resolving fundamental disagreements among the member nations.

Pakistan and India continued to compete as long as they were members of the South Asian Association for Regional Cooperation (SAARC). There has been fear and stress among the SAARC members due to the nuclear-armed confrontation between India and Pakistan. Despite the nations' desire to work together, the issues that remain unsolved prevent them from building confidence and expanding their collaboration. Because of India's dominant position in the area and Pakistan's wary attitude, SAARC was doomed from the start. Pakistan will not accept Indian domination, and India will not talk with Pakistan on an equal footing. The cancellation of the SAARC summit in Pakistan in November 2016 was due to the unfriendly attitude of both nations. Because of India's and other member nations' refusal to attend, the SAARC summit was called off. According to various diplomatic and political sources, Pakistan may not host the summit even in 2017. When India projected BIMSTEC as an alternative to SAARC, it was an attempt to diminish SAARC's importance in the eyes of Pakistan. As a result of India's efforts, the SAARC Summit slated for Pakistan was cancelled. In spite of the Indian government's intent to target and damage the Pakistani economy and alleviate poverty, these attempts instead harm the country's interests. As a result of these circumstances, Pakistan must address the issue of the Kashmir issue, its legal position on the water dispute, its sacrifices for the elimination of all forms of violence and terrorism, and its emphasis on unhindered cooperation that is essential for a balanced order in South Asia.

Pak-India Rivalry in the Context of SAARC

A lot of SAARC nations have tense ties with each other, which makes it difficult for them to cooperate and collaborate. It is impossible to overlook the importance of India's participation in this scenario of great distrust. The strategic importance of India in South Asia cannot be overstated[1]. Even

1. Kumar, R. (2014). SAARC: Changing Realities, Opportunities and Challenges. Retrieved from http://www.die-gdi.de/uploads/media/DP_11.2009.pdf

though India has had disagreements with various tiny countries in South Asia, these countries have since reconciled their ties with India. Today, India's position is more dominating than the small nations of South Asia save Pakistan. Since the partition of India into two separate states in 1947, Pakistan-India relations have remained tense. The ongoing competition between India and Pakistan is one of the key reasons SAARC is inefficient and prevents it from functioning as a subregional entity. The "Sword of Damocles" hanging over the efforts of South Asia to create regional stability and bring its actors closer together," as described by Tomislav Delinic[1]. In terms of economics, influence, population, and geographic position, India dominates the SAARC area. There was fear among the bordering nations because of India's intentions since every attempt to establish a free trade zone created worries within the Indian business sector, upsetting local businesses. The surrounding nations find India's foreign policy and the Indo-Sri Lanka Accord tiresome[2]. In addition, South Asia has several unresolved border and maritime conflicts. As a result of these unsolved issues, the SAARC nations have not only been unable to work together but have also been plagued by terrorism, smuggling, and a refugee crisis. The grouping was negatively affected by India and China's overlapping goals in the area. Sino-Sri Lanka and Sino-Bangladesh relations have established a distrust gap among SAARC members. In addition, Article X(2) of the SAARC charter provides for decisions on multilateral problems, limiting the potential for resolving bilateral conflicts. In light of these facts, it's possible that the group will disband. Although vibrant and aggressive, the organisation should explore the underlying reasons for regional disagreements and strive toward sensible solutions. In this regard, priority should be given to resolving basic concerns and restoring normalcy to ties between Pakistan and India.

The Cancellation of the SAARC Summit and its Impact on Pakistan's Foreign Policy

As time goes on, Pakistan's isolation on the regional and international fronts becomes more severe. For the most up-to-date news, check out the cancellation of the SAARC Summit scheduled for Pakistan in November 2016. By withdrawing from the SAARC Summit, India's departure has been ratified by Afghanistan, Bangladesh, and Bhutan. Non-participation

1. Deline, T. (2011). SAARC-25 Years of Regional Integration in South Asia. KAS International Reports.
2. Kaler, S. (2016). Successes and Failures Of SAARC: INDIAN JOURNAL OF APPLIED RESEARCH, 212-213.

in SAARC will dissolve if one member state refuses to participate. The withdrawal of five countries from the scheduled SAARC summit meeting in Pakistan shows the country's isolation in the region. Pakistan expressed displeasure with Bangladesh's strategy of executing war offenders from the 1971 conflict as a prelude to the country's exit. Afghanistan, Sri Lanka, and Bhutan announced their withdrawal from the SAARC Summit because of the recent rise in violence and terrorism. For this reason, India has withdrawn from the SAARC summit, according to the Indian foreign ministry: "increasing cross-border terrorist attacks in the region and growing interference in the internal affairs of member states by one country have created an environment that is not conducive to the successful holding of the 19th SAARC summit in Islamabad."[1]. Intimately linked to India, Bangladesh, Afghanistan, and a number of the other participants at the Saarc conference cancelled their attendance. According to Pakistan's foreign ministry reaction to India's decision, India aims to deflect global attention and human rights organisations away from its crimes and brutality in occupied Kashmir by obstructing the Saarc conference in Pakistan (Ibid). Pakistan's foreign policy and diplomacy have come under fire after the cancellation of the Saarc Summit. They contend that if India can work with the neighbouring countries and influence them to achieve its goals, why can't Pakistan?

Furthermore, the cancellation of the summit raises questions about the long-term viability of Saarc, given that it has been unable to demonstrate the value of its existence and still has no notable accomplishments to its name. According to Senator Sherry Rehman, a former Pakistani ambassador to the United States, Pakistan is in a precarious position regarding its foreign policy. The nation is now caught in the crosshairs of a perfect storm, with India, Afghanistan, and the United States all influencing it. Another front on which Pakistan's foreign policy apparatus failed to gain the confidence of regional governments was the abolition of SAARC. A major goal of foreign policy is to increase the number of friendly countries and decrease the number of enemy countries. As a result, Pakistan has lost allies and grown the number of those it considers an enemy. With each passing day, Pakistan's ties with its neighbours have worsened, save for China. Despite Pakistan's foreign policy leaders' best efforts, India won over Bangladesh, Iran, and Afghanistan.

1. Dawn. (2016, September 28). Saarc Summit in Pakistan was Postponed after the member states pulled out. Dawn News. Pakistan: http://www.dawn.com.

1.6.6 Sri Lanka

The word "resplendent" comes from the Sanskrit word "Lanka" (from the Pali "alankara"). Ancient stone tools discovered on the island date back 10 millennia or more, and evidence suggest plant domestication began about 1500 B.C. Because of its strategic position along old trade routes and the allure of Sri Lanka's "products," such as pearls, lumber, diamonds, ivory, and later spices, the island has long been a crossroads of East-West commerce. The Portuguese, Dutch, and British entrances in the 16th century marked the beginning of European naval supremacy. On February 4, 1948, Sri Lanka became an independent country. Sri Lanka has a population of 18.77 million people. This is a multicultural country. Seventy-four per cent of Sri Lanka's people are Sinhalese, while the island's 12.6% are Sri Lankan Tamils of Dravidian ancestry. Migrant labourers from South India were recruited by the British for 5.5 per cent of Indian Tamils in the past century. The Moors, ancestors of Arab merchants who landed on the island in the 12th century, make up 7.1% of the population. And 0.8 per cent of the population. The official languages of Sri Lanka are Sinhalese and Tamil, whereas English is the country's official language.[1].

Sri Lanka is where people of all faiths may freely practise their faiths. Buddhists make up 69.3% of the population, followed by Hindus (15.5%), Christians (7.5%), and Muslims (7.5%). Upon gaining sovereignty, Sri Lanka implemented the Westminster system, which established three branches of government: the Legislative Assembly, the Supreme Court, and a Cabinet led by the Prime Minister. A Governor General was appointed to serve as the island's official representative of the British monarchy, which remained in place as the country's constitutional head of state. Following an amendment to the Constitution in 1972, the British Crown was officially severed from the country. Since the 1978 modification to the Constitution, the country has been governed by an Executive Presidential form of government. Directly chosen by the people, the President serves a six-year term. A unicameral parliament with 225 members, selected using a proportional representation system, serves as the country's highest legislative body. Since there are several competing political parties, the country has a multi-party system. The Prime Minister is chosen from among the members of Parliament who represent the party with the most seats. Plantation products

1. Kripa, S. (2008). Regional Organisations and Conflict Management: Comparing ASEAN and SAARC, Working Paper 33 (Regional and Global Axes of Conflict), Singapore: Crisis States Research Centre, National University of Singapore, 12-15.

like tea and rubber were responsible for 90% of the country's economic output at independence. The economy has been gradually liberalised since the late 1970s. The transition in industrial strategy from import substitution to export-oriented manufacturing has occurred. Manufacturing currently makes up 16 per cent of GDP, agricultural is 21.1 per cent, building is 7.6 per cent, and mining makes up 1.9 per cent. Service presently makes up 52 per cent. Since the London auctions stopped operation in June 1998, Colombo has become the biggest Tea Auction Center in the world. Textiles and garments, coconut goods, spices, cocoa, coffee, essential oils, jewels, fisheries products, rubber, machinery, foot ware and leather items, and petroleum by-products are some of the other things exported from the Philippines.[1] Other major imports include crude oil, fertiliser and raw materials for construction, transportation, and machinery and equipment for manufacturing. Exports and imports were $5,459 million and $6,683 million in 2000; 10.11 per cent of the latter came from SAARC nations.

Many internal issues confront Sri Lanka and its neighbours in the South Asian Association of Regional Cooperation (SAARC). Because of the low levels of intra-regional trade and investment, the SAARC area has been deemed one of the world's least economically linked regions. Comparatively speaking, intra-regional trade in the East Asian, Southeast Asian, and Middle Eastern/African (MEA) regions amounts to approximately 35% of total trade. Still, in the SAARC area, it accounts for less than 5% of total official trade. The area failed to solidify its economic and geopolitical potential due to several factors. Still, despite these disparities, the region must actively work together to promote the well-being of its people and enhance their quality of life.

1.6.7 Nepal

The documented history of Nepal begins with the Changu Narayan Temple Inscription of King Manadeva I (464 AD), followed by the Malla rulers, among other notables. Before the emergence of Nepal as a unified nation in the second half of the eighteenth century, the name Nepal applied only to the Kathmandu Valley. Nepal was divided into more than 52 small principalities. Prithvi Narayan Shah, the great king of Gorkha, was the creator of modern Nepal, who unified the country in 1769 by conquering

1. Niazi, Tarique. 2014. —Ecological Disasters: The Political Economy of Floods in Pakistan. A conference paper presented at the World Congress of Sociology in Yokohama, Japan.

the Kathmandu Valley and making it the capital. Nepal has a population of about 23.9 million, comprising 61 ethnic groups living in different regions, speaking 70 languages and dialects. Nepali is the national language. Hinduism is the official religion of Nepal, and Hindus make up more than 85% of the population. Buddha, the founder of Buddhism, was born in Nepal around 563 BC, and Buddhists make up 7.8% of the population. A small minority of Nepalese profess Islam and Christianity. After 1951, Nepal practised multi-party democracy except for about three decades, from 1961 to 1990, when there was a panchayat system without parties. But again, after the democratic movement of 1990, Nepal restored a multi-party system with a constitutional monarchy. His Majesty the King is the head of state, and the Prime Minister serves as the head of government. According to the Constitution, there are two houses of Parliament, namely Pratinidhi Sabha (House of Representatives) and Rashtriya Sabha (National Assembly). The House of Representatives consists of 205 members elected by the people for five-year terms. National.

The Assembly consists of 60 members, 10 of whom are nominated by His Majesty the King. At the same time, the remaining 50 are elected, 35 by members of the Pratinidhi Sabha and 15 by members of local bodies. Nepal's economy is agriculture, which accounts for 41% of the GDP, and over 80% of the people depend on it. The main crops grown are paddy, maise and wheat. Manufacturing, trade and tourism follow agriculture as the country's main economic activities. Hand-knitted woollen carpets and ready-made garments are a thriving industry in the country, accounting for nearly 32 per cent of total exports. Petroleum products, chemicals and drugs, food and live animals, vehicles, machinery and equipment, are the main imports from Nepal.

As a South Asian Regional Cooperation member, Nepal has always sought to protect its identity, position, and economic independence. He underlined in August 1983 that "SAARC will be built on the basis of equality, respect of sovereignty and territorial integrity," non-interference, and mutuality of interest 1950. Nepal also set up SAARC in order to reduce India's influence in the area.

As far as forming alliances is concerned, Nepal is firmly rooted in reality. There is a security problem for tiny governments like Nepal, as Goetschel (1998) noted. Nepal does not wish to be trampled by India and Pakistan, the two antagonists of South Asia. Likewise, India and China, Nepal wants to progress economically and socially but doesn't want to be seen as naive or misguided. Consequently, Nepal desires goodwill and the preservation of its right to conduct itself without interference.

While much has been written on Nepal's foreign policy, there is a lack of information about the country's relationship with regional organisations. SAARC is the most significant regional body for Nepal. Despite this, experts have shown little enthusiasm for delving more into the function of SAARC's smaller member nations. Therefore, the chapter explores the tactics and possibilities for a tiny South Asian state like Nepal to handle its concerns better to comprehend Nepal and its significant role in regional organisations. An overview of theoretical notions about tiny states and the security dynamics that come with them, which are vastly different from those of their bigger counterparts, is also provided in this chapter.

Located in Asia's subregion, Nepal is a landlocked state that shares borders with the countries of China, India, and Bangladesh. It has a population of almost 27 million people living over an area of 56,827 square miles. Nepal is a "little state" compared to its massive neighbours, geographically and in terms of people. Nonetheless, it's an arbitrary classification since there's no defined scale for determining how tiny an area or population of a state is. Many factors are not considered when determining whether a state is "large or tiny," such as political and economic strength and influence. However, it serves as a decent descriptor of a tiny state. In Peter Katzenstein's view, the fundamental distinction between small and big states is "the extent of their territory and the magnitude of their activity."

In contrast, there are several ways to describe a tiny state. According to Clive Archer, Alyson Bailes, and Anders Wivel (2014), "a weaker portion of an unequal connection, which is unable to modify the character or functioning of the partnership on its own."[1]. Similarly, Jaquet (1971) claims that "a small state is a state that is neither on a global nor regional scale to impose its political will or protect its national interests by exerting power politics". Talukder Manruzzaman writes, "A small state's goal is not the pursuit of power but the preservation of the little power it possesses."[2]. In contrast, there are several ways to describe a tiny state. According to Clive Archer, Alyson Bailes, and Anders Wivel (2014), "a weaker portion of an

1. Bailes and A. Wivel (2014), the Small States and International Security: Europe and Beyond, Routledge: Abingdon.
2. Maniruzzaman, Talukder (1982), The Security of Small States in the Third World, The Australian National University: Canberra.

unequal connection, which is unable to modify the character or functioning of the partnership on its own."[1].

When it comes to long-term international friendships, a policy of autonomy or neutrality has a detrimental impact. Autonomy policy has disappeared in today's multipolar realpolitik, which prioritises power balance and bandwagoning tactics to avoid large-scale global confrontations. With their tiny size and limited resources, small nations rely heavily on regional and international interactions to maintain their self-assertive character. According to Rothstein (1969), tiny nations cannot achieve security independently and must rely on the assistance of larger governments and organisations. When it comes to multilateral diplomacy and interdependency, small governments have a strong affinity for it. The creation of alliances helps tiny nations share burdens and pool resources. Alliances and summits provide a forum for tiny nations to express their concerns and ideas.

Bandwagoning or maintaining a power balance has its problems, of course. In the long run, the state's well-being is linked to its commitment to a particular grouping. Nepal has expanded its network of contacts as a member of several regional and international organisations. However, this has also reduced the likelihood of Nepal adopting an abandoning policy in the name of national interest and security. Nepal's sovereignty is thus vulnerable to the country's internal political and economic changes and its relationships with countries beyond its boundaries.

Nepal was the founder of the South Asian Association for Regional Cooperation (SAARC), which signed its charter in 1985. Nepal was selected to host the SAARC Secretariat in 1987 after it was approved by the other founding members. South Asia's economic progress, social peace, and the welfare of its citizens are all goals of the South Asian Association for Regional Cooperation (SAARC). Nepal should ideally benefit from its position as head of SAARC's Secretariat office, yet the issue remains: Does Nepal have substantial influence in SAARC?

Even though the SAARC mandate gives equal weight to all eight member states, it is indisputable that the interaction between India and Pakistan, the two South Asian powers, decides how and what the structure

1. Dahl, Ann Sofie (1997), "To Be or Not To Be Neutral: Swedish Security Strategy in the Post-Cold War Era", in Efraim Inbar and Gabriel Sheffer (eds.) The National Security of Small States in a Changing World, Frank Cass Publishers: London/ Portland.

and authority of SAARC will be. Some claim that tiny governments are incapable of implementing significant policy changes in organisations because of their limited size. As a member of SAARC, Pakistan has been the most sluggish and has provided the least support for its growth and expansion. Since SAARC has not been able to enhance its working circumstances despite the rest of its members' best efforts to lead it towards progress and better collaboration during the last three decades. The capacity of tiny governments like Nepal, Bhutan, the Maldives, and Sri Lanka to move within a regional coalition's structural difficulties is hampered in such a setting. However, the regional cooperation strategy will continue despite the political obstacles and ill will. Nepal has opted to broaden its allegiance beyond SAARC to other regional and sub-regional groups that attempt to fill the holes in SAARC, continuing the trend towards regionalism in South Asia. There are two such alliances that assist speed up economic ties between South Asian and Southeast Asian countries: the Bay of Bengal Initiative for Multi-Sectoral Technical and Economic Cooperation (BIMSTEC) and BBIN (an abbreviation for Bangladesh, Bhutan, India, and Nepal).

1.6.8 Afghanistan

Afghanistan is a landlocked country in Southern Asia that borders China, Iran, Pakistan, Tajikistan, Turkmenistan, and Uzbekistan. The geography of Afghanistan is arid and mountainous; the Hindu Kush Mountains run northeast to southwest and divide the northern provinces from the rest of the country. The government system is the Islamic Republic; the chief of state and head of government is the President. Afghanistan has a controlled economic system in which the central government directs the economy regarding the production and distribution of goods.[1]

Afghanistan has shown keen interest in joining the South Asian Association for Regional Cooperation (SAARC) since its inception in 1985; civil war and political instability have proved obstacles to becoming part of the regional group. Only 23 years after the establishment of SAARC, Afghanistan became one of its members during the 14th SAARC Summit in New Delhi in 2007.

After the fall of the Taliban regime and the formation of a government, strengthening regional cooperation by maintaining cordial relations with

1. Afghanistan: Introduction Retrieved on September 23, 2022, from: https://globaledge.msu.edu/countries/afghanista

neighbouring South Asian countries became an important approach to Afghanistan's foreign policy. Having great relations with SAARC member states is paramount for the country as it will help achieve peace and stability through better trade and regional connectivity. All SAARC member states, especially India and Pakistan, welcome Afghanistan as its strategic location is key to economic development. Afghanistan acts as a gateway to West Asia and Central Asia for South Asian countries, a significant factor for SAARC's economic cooperation and energy security agenda. According to unexplored natural gas reserves, it is home to $1 trillion (U.S.) worth of minerals. It also has an unexplored resource base such as iron, nickel, chromium, copper, silver, gold, sulphur, magnesium, mica, mercury, bauxite, lithium and ruby. Energy-deficit economies are, therefore, impatiently waiting for the stabilisation of the country in order to access these resources. Indian and Chinese companies have already become huge players in Afghanistan's raw materials markets, especially in the oil sector.

In addition to economic and trade cooperation, Afghanistan faces security challenges similar to those of its neighbours and other SAARC countries. Terrorism, poverty and illiteracy are prominent in all SAARC countries. While terrorism is at an all-time high, illiteracy and poverty have been reduced but not eradicated. These problems are better solved when they are worked on together. Afghanistan has functioned as a breeding ground for terrorism, impacting the nation and its neighbours and disrupting peace and security in the international community. Therefore, to find credible solutions to eradicate terrorism, cooperation through SAARC is essential for both the region and Afghanistan. Afghanistan has acted as a breeding ground for terrorism, affecting the nation and its neighbours and disrupting peace and security in the international community.

Almost all SAARC member states are developing countries, each trying to expand its sphere of influence. However, in the last decade or so, countries have come to understand that cooperation can facilitate their rise as an essential regional bloc; to assert their influence on the international scene. The cooperation has hosted nineteen summits since its inception, none hosted by Afghanistan due to financial and security concerns. However, despite the challenges, Afghanistan has fully engaged within its capabilities. It organised some important meetings like SAFTA (South Asian Free Trade Agreement) in October 2015 and contributed to building South Asian University along with other South Asian countries. Social and developmental projects such as maternal and child health care have benefited the country after its investment in the SAARC fund.[1]

The situation in Afghanistan is constantly changing, and the war-torn country's future seems uncertain, especially if the troops withdraw and a government friendly to the Taliban is installed. Regardless of the support of international donors, there may be a decrease in funds or aid intended for the development of Afghanistan. Kabul will need to tap into other sources of revenue to stabilise its crumbling economy, deteriorating security and collapsing society. In this scenario, its immediate neighbours and SAARC can help provide support as the changing dynamics affect their stability and peace.

1.7 Summits of SAARC

SAARC First Summit:

The First SAARC Summit took place on 7-8 December 1985 in Dhaka, Bangladesh. The First Summit authorised the creation of a study group by the Standing Committee to investigate the issue of terrorism, as it affects the security and stability of SAARC Member States. It also agreed to do a similar exercise on the issue of drug trafficking and misuse.

The Second Summit of SAARC:

In Bangalore, India, the Second SAARC Summit convened on 16-17 November 1986. The second SAARC summit approved for the establishment of the South Asian Broadcasting Programme. The Heads of State and Government have placed emphasis on connections between people and on tangible measures for facilitating tourism in the area, including restricted convertibility facilities for SAARC nations visitors in their national currencies.

The Heads of State and Government have again stressed the significance they regard to the easy availability of students, scholars and researchers from their respective nations to accurate and up-to-date technical, scientific and development information. A SAARC Documentation Center as a repository of such knowledge may best fulfil this requirement.

---

1. Krupa Vasani, "Afghanistan's Re-integration in SAARC" Retrieved on September 25, 2022, from - https://jgu-dev.s3.ap-south-1.amazonaws.com/Afghanistans-Re-integration-in-SAARC.pdf.

SAARC Third Summit:

The South Asian Regional Cooperation Association (SAARC) Third Summit was held in Kathmandu, Nepal on November 2-4, 1987.

The Kathmandu Declaration offered a fresh path and direction for South Asia's future development of regional Cooperation.

The SAARC Summit also said that it intends to launch a process to address the causes and effects of natural disasters and resolved to begin, in a well-planned and comprehensive manner, research on natural disasters, environmental protection and protection.

SAARC Fourth Summit:

The Fourth Summit of the South Asian Regional Cooperation Association took place on 29-31 December 1988 in Islamabad, Pakistan.

Members agreed to designate 1989 as the SAARC Year Against Drug Abuse, with the aim of concentrating attention on drug-related issues in the region. They urged Member States to develop and execute national programmes. It also agreed to designate 1990 the Girl Child's SAARC Year.

SAARC Fifth Summit:

From 21-23 November 1990, the Fifth Summit of the South Asian Association for Regional Cooperation was held in Male, Maldives.

During the first half of 1991, the SAARC Summit began the programme for the promotion of organised tourism. Members also applauded the idea for structured collaboration between Member States' tourism sectors in order to attract more visitors from outside the area.

The Heads of State and government stressed the importance of Cooperation between SAARC member states in the area of mass media and led the Secretary-General to facilitate the increased interaction between federations/associations of journalists, news agencies and the region's mass media under the auspices of SAARC.

The years 1991 to 2000 A.D. were recognised as the girl Child's SAARC Decade. They were profoundly affected by the call for love and care for them and their right to childhood made by the SAARC Girl Child. They reaffirmed their determination that the kid's well-being in general and the girl's child in particular would be at the top of their priority list.

The 1991 Summit was also designated the SAARC Year of Shelter. They chose to mark 1992 as the "Year of Environment" for SARC.

Moreover, the 1993 SAARC Summit also agreed to commemorate the SAARC Year of Persons with Disabilities.

SAARC members agreed furthermore that suitable programmes to observe the SAARC Shelter Year of 1991, the SAARC Year of Environment of 1992 and the SAARC Year of People with Disabilities of 1993 should be developed.

Sixth Summit of SAARC:

On 21 December 1991, the Sixth SAARC Summit was convened on the Declaration of the Heads of State or Government of the Member States of the South Asian Regional Cooperation Association, released by Mr Colombo.

The SAARC Member States also referred to the Malé Summit's resolution to institutionalise biotechnology cooperation. They praised the idea for a networking arrangement between research and development centres in the Member States as an essential step to promote this collaboration. They also appreciated the focus on planned tours, workshops and seminars in the areas of science and technology collaboration selected[1].

SAARC Seventh Summit:

The South Asian Regional Cooperation Association (SAARC) Seventh Summit was held in Dhaka, Bangladesh on 10-11 April 1993. The Member States have again reiterated the need to strengthen and enrich SAARC as an instrument that gives it clear objectives and goals and all the institutional capacities needed for the future and so that it can continue to work on not only enriching its own members' lives, but also on promoting peace, advancement and stability in South Asia in a broader context.

SAARC Eighth Summit:

South Asian Regional Cooperation Association (SAARC) Eighth Summit was held in New Delhi, India, on 2-4 May 1995.

The Member States underlined the need to meet the globally agreed assistance goals for developing countries and L.D.C.s. They underlined

1. Agrawal P., P. Sahoo and R J Dash (2010) Savings Behavior in India: Co-integration and Causality Evidence, Singapore Economic Review, 55, 2, 273-95.

the need for special funding to assist the execution of SAARC countries' economic reform plans.

Ninth Summit of SAARC:

The Ninth Summit of the South Asian Regional Cooperation Association (SAARC) was held on 12 -14 May 1997 in Malé, Maldives.

The SAARC Member States agreed that they should review the criteria for determining the status of the L.D.C. for consideration by the General Assembly of the United Nations for this year, taking into account the particular importance of the scale and magnitude of poverty in the poorest countries and the particular vulnerabilities of small island states.

SAARC Tenth Summit:

From 29 to31 July 1998, at the Golden Jubilee of Independence in Sri Lanka, the 10th summit of the South Asian Association for Regional Cooperation (SAARC) took place in Colombo.

The SAARC Member States reaffirmed their commitment to a fair, durable, and comprehensive peace based on Security Council Resolutions 242 (1967) and 338 (1973), which would restore Palestinians' inherent national rights.

SAARC Eleventh Summit:

On 4-6 January 2002, the eleventh conference of the South Asian Association of Regional Cooperation (SAARC) took place in Kathmandu, Nepal.

The Heads of State and Government unanimously acknowledged the need to further promote the feeling of regional identity among the peoples of the area. The leaders praised the role of intellectuals, professionals and prominent individuals in fostering connections amongst people in the area and decided to promote such initiatives as a good indication of regional cohesiveness and brotherhood.

SAARC Twelfth Summit:

On 4-6 January 2004, the Twelfth Meeting of the South Asian Association for Regional Cooperation (SAARC) was place in Islamabad, Pakistan. The 12th Summit was driven by a vision for South Asia that was peaceful and wealthy and proud of its rich culture and traditions.

Member States wanted to promote peace, stability, friendship and progress in the region by strict adherence to the principles of the Charter and non-alignment of the United Nations, in particular respect for the principles of sovereign equality, territorial integrality, national independence, non-utilisation of force and non-interference in the internal affairs of states and peaceful settlement[1].

The Thirteenth SAARC Summit:

On 12-13 November 2005, the 13th Summit meeting of the Association of South Asian Regional Cooperation (SAARC) took place in Dhaka, Bangladesh.

The Heads of State and Government agreed to proclaim a decade of poverty alleviation for 2006-2015 as the SAARC Decade. Over the decade, efforts will continue to be undertaken at national and regional level, with a feeling of dedication and urgency to get South Asia out of poverty.

The Heads of State and Government underlined the need to maintain the spirit of SAARC via efforts to encourage interpersonal relations and across South Asia, a dynamic civil society actively engaged in building connections across national borders.

The Fourteenth SAARC Summit:

The 14th Summit of the South Asian Regional Cooperation Association (SAARC) was held in New Delhi, India, on 3-4 April 2007.

The SAARC countries welcomed the new membership of the Islamic Republic of Afghanistan. The SAARC Car Rally was a strong symbol of this connection in the run-up to the 14th SAARC Summit.

The 15th SAARC Summit:

The South Asian Association for Regional Co-operation (SAARC) Fifteenth Summit conference took place in Colombo, Sri Lanka on 2-3 August 2008.

The SAARC members reaffirmed their determination to collectively support regional economic growth, social advancement and cultural development to foster the wellness and quality of life of the peoples of South Asia, thus contributing to peace, stability, friendship and progress in the area.

1. Bhagwati J. and T. N. Srinivasan (2002) Trade and Poverty in the Poor Countries, American Economic Review, 92: 2: May: 180-183

The SAARC mechanisms should continue to incorporate and concentrate in their plans on improved connectivity not just within South Asia, but also between the region and the rest of the globe[1].

The Sixteenth SAARC Summit:

The sixteenth Summit of the South Asian Regional Cooperation Association (SAARC) took place from 28 to 29 April 2010 in Thimphu, Bhutan, with the theme Towards Greenery and Happy South Asia to celebrate the silver anniversary.

In this Silver Jubilee Year of the SAARC, the leaders stressed that a vision statement must be developed.

The SAARC members emphasised efficient communication and public diplomacy in celebration of the 25th anniversary. It also supported the recommendation that 2010-2020 be declared under the SAARC Decade of Intra-regional Connectivity. Furthermore, it was agreed on the necessity to accelerate talks to conclude the two Motor Vehicle and Railway Agreements.

The 17th SAARC Summit:

The 17th meeting of the South Asian Association for Regional Cooperation (SAARC) took place in Addu City, Maldives, on 10-11 November, 2011

In the first speech, Maldivian President Mohamed Nasheed stated that economic stagnation creates instability in one country in another. Nasheed also called for economic integration and the creation of a secure political environment.

At the opening ceremony of the seventeenth SAARC Summit, Yousuf Raza Gilani, Pakistani Prime Minister, appealed on all SAARC countries to work together to eradicate terrorism.

Indian Prime Minister Manmohan Singh has committed to promoting fair commerce in the area. Dr Singh further pointed out that it has been beneficial to several areas, including commerce, transportation, health and education[2].

1. Bhattarai K. (2010) Strategic and general equilibrium models of poverty, Romanian Journal of Economic Forecasting, 13;1:137-150
2. Bhattarai K. and S. Mallick (2013) Impact of Chinais currency valuation and labour cost on the U.S. in a trade and exchange rate model. North American Journal of Economics and Finance, 25:40-59

South Asia has kept its growth rates respectable and this positive trend has led to SAARC integration and indicates that the region is on the right road, said Singh.

At the concluding speech, the SAARC Member States decided to instruct SAFTA's Ministerial Council (South Asian Free Trade Agreement) to step up efforts to decrease the sensitive list and eliminate non-tariff obstacles to trade.

Maldivian President Mohamed Nasheed stated that the SAARC Secretary General was asked to guarantee the final preparations were completed this year for the Indian Ocean cargo and the Passenger Ferry Service.

Nasheed added the other measures to enhance communication among SAARC nations have also been undertaken. The Summit decided to complete the Regional Railway Agreement and hold before the next Council of Ministers the Expert Group Meeting on the Motor Vehicles Agreement. In addition, it was decided to set up a South Asian Postal Union, Nasheed stated.

The 17th SAARC Summit concluded Friday, 11 November 2011, with the acceptance by the eight nations of the SAARC of the Addu Declaration, which reaffirmed their commitment to peace, developing trust, freedom, dignity, democracy, mutual respect, good governance and human rights.

The President of the 17th SAARC Summit and the President of the Maldives, Mohamed Nasheed, has declared officially that the 18th SAARC Summit would take place in Nepal.

The 18th SAARC Summit:

The 18th SAARC Summit was held at the Nepalese capital Kathmandu from 26 November to 27 November, 2014 and was attended by the prime ministers of Bangladesh, Bhutan, India, Nepal and Pakistan, and the presidents of the Afghanistan, Maldives and Sri Lanka. The motto was 'Deeper Integration for Peace and Prosperity. The legal permission on SAARC Satellite Scheme was in this summit. The scheme will be developed in all member nations except Bangladesh and Pakistan.

The 19th SAARC Summit:

Pakistan was scheduled to host the 19th summit of the South Asian Association for Regional Cooperation (SAARC) in Islamabad on 15 to 16

November 2016. Following the 2016 Uri terror attack, India cancelled its participation in the 19th SAARC summit, alleging Pakistan's involvement in the terror attack.

1.8 SAARC Regional Centres

Since 1989, a number of regional centers have been established with specific mandates to strengthen and support regional Cooperation. Regional centers implement program activities and are expected to develop into centers of excellence in their respective fields. These centers are governed by governing boards composed of representatives from all member states, the Secretary General of SAARC and the Ministry of Foreign Affairs/External Affairs of the host government. The director of the center acts as a member secretary of the administrative board, which is subordinate to the Program Committee.

SAARC Agriculture Centre (S.A.C.), Dhaka

This center was established in 1989 with the mandate to provide timely, relevant and universal access to information and knowledge resources to all agricultural professionals of SAARC member countries to achieve their respective objectives through linkage of agricultural knowledge and information systems by adopting appropriate information and communication technology, management practices and standards.[1]

SAARC Energy Centre (S.E.C.), Islamabad

This center was established in 2006 with a mandate to envision itself as a catalyst for the economic growth and development of the South Asian region by initiating, coordinating and supporting regional as well as joint and joint energy activities. The S.E.C. would provide technical inputs to the SAARC Working Group (and others) meetings on energy and help accelerate the integration of energy strategies within the region by providing relevant information, state-of-the-art technology and expertise.[2]

SAARC Cultural Centre (SCC), Colombo, Sri Lanka

This center was established in 2009 with a mandate to promote regional unity through cultural integration and intercultural dialogue and to

1. SAARC Secretariat Retrieved 21 September, 2022, from https://www.saarc-sec.org/index.php/regional-centres
2. SAARC Energy Centre (S.E.C.), Islamabad. (n.d.). Retrieved 21 September, 2022, from https://www.saarcenergy.org/

contribute to the conservation, preservation and protection of the cultural heritage of South Asia under the SAARC Program for Culture.[1]

SAARC Tuberculosis and HIV/AIDS Centre (STAC), Kathmandu

This center was established in 1992 with the mandate to prevent and control tuberculosis in the region by coordinating the efforts of the national T.B. programs of the Member States; information exchange, research, capacity building and implementation activities; collects, compiles, analyses and disseminates information on the latest developments and findings in the field of tuberculosis in the region and elsewhere.[2]

SAARC Disaster Management Centre (SDMC), India

This center was reconstituted in November 2016 for an expanded role by merging four former SAARC centres, viz. (1) SAARC Disaster Management Center (SDMC – New Delhi, India); (2) SAARC Meteorological Research Center (SMRC – Dhaka, Bangladesh); (3) SAARC Forestry Center (S.F.C. – Thimphu, Bhutan); (4) SAARC Coastal Zone Management Center (SCZMC – Male, Maldives) with a mandate to support Member States in their disaster risk reduction initiatives through the application of science and technology, cross-disciplinary knowledge, exchange of best practices, capacity development, collaborative research and networking in accordance with global priorities / goals and other relevant frameworks adopted by Member States[3].

1.9 SAARC Achievements

SAFTA

SAARC introduced (South Asian Free Trade Area (SAFTA) to boost trade among member states and in December 1995, emphasising the need to understand the "South Asian Free Zone Exchange" (SAFTA). The treaty was signed at the 12th summit held in Islamabad. In December 2005, the Indian government approved SAFTA, marking it for its official launch on 1 January 2006, when it was hoped that all participating countries would reduce interest rates by the 2016 deadline.

1. SAARC Cultural Centre Retrieved 21 September, 2022, from saarcculture.org
2. SAARC TB and HIV/AIDS Centre | STAC Retrieved 21 September, 2022, from https://www.saarctb.org/
3. SAARC Disaster Management Centre (I.U.) Retrieved 21 September, 2022, http://saarc-sdmc.org/

South Asian Identity

The most important achievements of SAARC are to bring member states together and think about regional issues and identity. This is based on the positive aspect of the individual state, which should be attractive for the people of SAARC countries to emulate. It is important not to think like a South Asian, but to be proud of the South Asian identity within the region. There is also a serious need for people-to-people Cooperation and contact, improving cultural identity and breaking barriers between people in the South.[1]

The SAARC Food Bank

The "SAARC Food Bank" was initially recognised as an emergency resource to address shortage crisis or natural disasters, floods, earthquakes and similar other problems. At the 14th Summit in Islamabad, they signed a channel to adopt a mutual position to unify "food security" for the people of South Asia, and then formal development and progress for strategies must plan ahead to provide a functional character[2]

SAARC Development Fund

The SAARC Development Fund was recognised by the eight SAARC members in 2010. The objective of the S.D.F. was to "promote well-being for the people of the South Asian region; improve their quality of life, economic growth, social progress and poverty". It is also one of the achievements of the Regional Association for Security, Progress and Prosperity for the People of South Asia.

South Asian University

The South Asian University is another achievement by the members' state. it is an international university established in 2010 by the SAARC desk. At this time University is offering postgraduate and doctoral programs in several disciplines. "While SAARC may constantly be engaged in resolving the political and economic dilemmas amongst its members with limited success, optimists view the Cooperation on education as one of the few achievements of SAARC. It may also be a catalyst for the regional

1 Pattanaik, S. (2011). South Asia: Envisioning a Regional Future. New Delhi, Pentagon Security International

2. SAARC Summit. (2011). SAARC Food Bank: Will It Be Enough Broad-Based, People's Campaign on 17th SAARC Summit, House 13/3, Road 2, Shamoli Dhaka -1207, Bangladesh.

integration process. The university aims to create a center of excellence and produce leaders who identify themselves as citizens of the region with a common vision of success for both their home country and the neighbors"[1].

SAARC Arbitration Council

The arbitration council is an achievement of SAARC to provide a legal forum for the South Asian nations for solving conflicts. "SAARC Arbitration Council, Islamabad, is one of the Specialized Bodies of South Asian Association for Regional Co-operation; comprising the eight-member StatesSAARC arbitration council is an inter-governmental body authorised to provide a legal framework or forum within the region for fair and effective settlement of industrial, commercial, trade, investment banking, such their other issues, and disputes, as may be referred to it by the member states and their people"[2].

South Asian Regional Standards Organization

The Establishment of SARSO entered with effect from 25 August 2011 after approval by all SAARC countries. Through the creation of the (SARSO) in 2011, "a particular body to deal with trade-related standards, here is major potential for greater coordination of such standards to support trade growth in South Asia and universally for SAARC countries. By reviewing other relevant standardisation organisations, their methods and achievements, SARSO can adopt the tools and necessary approaches to achieve its goals and those of SAARC. The SARSO is positioned to create strong and effective structures for the harmonisation of trade standards to facilitate economic growth and development in South Asia"[3]

1.10 Challenges of SAARC

The dangers to India's environment for peace and security have increased tremendously, just as the threat to global peace is darker and menacing today. The balance of regional and international powers is threateningly hostile. The worst, the most dreadful crisis confronting India now is the nuclear option.

---

1. Dogra, S. (2010). South Asian University: Catalyst for Regional Cooperation?Institute of South Asian Studies.
2. SAARC Summit. (2011). SAARC Food Bank: Will It Be Enough Broad-Based, People's Campaign on 17th SAARC Summit, House 13/3, Road 2, Shamoli Dhaka -1207, Bangladesh.
3. Cote, K.R. (2016). A Proposed Agenda for the South Asian Regional Standards Organisation. Jaipur, Centre for International Trade, Economics & Environment

Indo-Pak collaboration was an integral aspect of the South Asian endeavour at the international level to create a coordinated and determined drive for mutual development. In the beginning India took a little part out of concern that smaller neighbours would be suspected of it, but Bangladesh and Nepal showed more effort. The Foreign Secretaries of the seven South Asian countries (Nepal, Bangladesh, Sri Lanka, Pakistan, Bhutan, The Maldives and India) met in Colombo in early 1981 to promote mutual Cooperation in the areas that will benefit the whole region and set up cooperation studies groups for agriculture, rural development, meteorology, public health and telecommunications. Some 13 initiatives in these areas were selected by the working groups. In Kathmandu in November 1981, the second conference of the Foreign Ministers broadened the scope of regional Cooperation by studying three additional projects: postal services, science and technology and transportation. The conference in Kathmandu provided the much-needed stimulus and expedited the process of establishing a shared basis for collaboration[1].

Apart from the huge economic challenges, the South Asian area was affected by numerous political concerns. The legacies of mistrust, sometimes bitterness, were too great to be simply rejected. Regional collaboration could clearly not immediately assume the shape of political Cooperation. However, history's lesson was as obvious. Either collaborate and go forward together or suffer individually and independently. South Asia had to discover a path to regional Cooperation which would not disregard regional realities and thus not suffer early death. In order to create a better basis for resolving political difficulties, this route had to start necessarily by becoming the path of economic Cooperation. The process was barely underway, and it was too early to tell whether it might be swamped by political instability or controlled by political upheaval. The politicians, bureaucrats and intellectuals were in reality responsible for ensuring, consolidating and continuing the regional cooperation process for all of the people in these nations.

The link between national and foreign policy is a key feature in the development of foreign policy, whether it is in India or in any other country. This should not lead us to think that ideas play no part. Ideas and even ideas have their place and you don't have to snack them. Unintended pursuit of what may be perceived to be urgent can frequently be counterproductive[2].

1. Brandt L, D Ma, T. G. Rawski (2014) From Divergence to Convergence: Reevaluating the History Behind Chinaís Economic Boom, Journal of Economic Literature 52:1, 45-123
2. Dedola Luca, Peter Karadi, Giovanni Lombardo (2013) Global implications of national unconventional policies, Journal of Monetary Economics, 60, 1, 66-85

External policy is not morality. It is not morality. In general, foreign policy stumbles and is greatly affected by the experience of a nation. Perhaps we can even generalise that foreign policy is the culmination of the experience of a particular country's international relations at a certain stage. It is certainly the real experience of India which has decided whether ties with one nation are better and somewhat indifferent, with one power more friends and with another less friendly. The existing condition of ties with other nations is mainly the function and result of experience.

A large nation like India should be able to maintain some initiative and demonstrate a certain dynamism with regard to events beyond its boundaries and across the globe, not simply a reactive foreign policy. Try to minimise current tensions without losing old friendships and explore new alternatives. To the degree that India can pursue this strategy energetically and with greater complexity, it can face the growing difficulties in a harder and colder world.

Historical causes and many more variables lead to non-cooperation in SAARC nations. The political differences as well as the mutual suspicion and lack of trust are the greatest enemies of SAARC cooperation, Kashmir between India and Pakistan, the water and refugee disputes between India and Bangladesh, India's involvement in Sri Lankan military, trade and transit treaty between India and Nepal, and Bhutan and North ethnic differences.

SAARC nations are are compelled and intra-competitive for political reasons that override the economic ones. Examples include India and Sri Lanka rivalry for tea export, jute market competitions between India and Bangladesh, India/Pakistan competition for rice export, Pakistan/Sri Lanka global market competition for cotton textiles. India is the dominant country of the SAARC nations towards India as regards region, population, technical development and military activities, which may lead to a steady and gradual expansion of Cooperation between the SAARC countries. The religious and cultural issues also hamper the development of SAARC to some degree. Economic and cultural collaboration with Islamic nations is preferable to a country like Pakistan; Nepal and Bhutan are spiritually and culturally closer to India, since these countries are dominated by Hindu and Buddhist faiths[1]. There are also differing economic fears that India

1. Fama E.F. (2014) Two Pillars of Asset Pricing, American Economic Review, 104(6): 1467-1485

and Pakistan are more evolved and developed than Bhutan, Nepal and the Maldives when they are exploited by more comparably developed allies.

Although there is a lack of confidence and mistrust that irritates one another, there is still a wide potential for SAARC-cooperation. Agriculture must be the emphasis of the SAARC nations. Agriculture is the only path forward and Cooperation is because those nations have core expertise in this area and agriculture dominates their economy as well. There must always be efforts to eliminate the main irritants in India's political and economic dominance of mutual fear. The finest method and the need of the hour is to be honest with sincerity and honesty. The SAARC Countries must understand that we can swim over the tumultuous river in collaboration, while separately drowning even in calm waters.

Nuclearisation as Challenge for South Asia

In May 1998, the Indian nuclear test led Pakistan to do nuclear testing, both of which resulted in becoming considered nuclear weapons States (N.W.S.). Again in 2001, in Kargil, the Indian Armed Forces branded Pakistan a 'Operation Poorna Vijay,' which encouraged the atmosphere of nuclear war.

In addition, terrorism has added a new dimension to the nuclear issue which may be referred to as two-stage issues. Terrorist activists disrupted the nation and its neighbourhood states' peaceful Cooperation. As on 26 November 2008, terrorist activities in Mumbai are creating trauma and unconducive surroundings in the nation.

Pakistan is controlled by military forces with profound fanaticism. Pakistan's nuclear strategy remains open, unlike New Delhi's no-first-use doctrine (NFU).

India has a nuclear "minimum credible deterrence" policy. Yet, miscalculations and adventurism in many nations would cost both opponents dearly.

Great cooperation potential

There is tremendous potential for regional collaboration amongst the countries of South Asia. Since the establishment of the SAARC in 1985, there have been discussions about future collaboration among them from time to time. In twelve domains, the scope of regional collaboration was identified: (i) agriculture; (ii) health and rural development; (iii) meteorology;

(vi) postal services; (vi) transport; (vii) scientific/technological development; (viii) sport; (ix) art and culture; (x) drug prevention and misuse; (xi) women and development; and (xi) training.

The same issues of poverty, unemployment, inflationary pressure, the unfavourable trade balance, large budget deficits and poor growth rates are typically experienced among the SAARC nations. Despite similar issues, the measures chosen are mutually contradictory. The problems of policy were more competitive than complementary or cooperative. It stemmed from historical realities that it was preferable to solve their issues through competing[1].

The countries of South Asia were connected to developed economic countries through assistance and commerce. SAARC nations pulled SAARC countries into the Western industrialised countries like foreign currency, advanced technology, and foreign assistance. In the early phases of economic growth money and technological support from industrialised countries were scarce.

The developed world pushes the third-world countries like SAARC to unite in various forums, such as the W.T.O., Globe Bank, I.M.F. etc., and expand their negotiating strength with industrialised nations of the world, where more concessions may be made by a regional block rather than a single country. It has forced South Asia to establish SAARC for economic, social and political progress.

The SAARC nations have finally recognised that they are working together in order to address their issues of poverty, unemployment, inflation and poor growth. Mutual dread and apprehension to improve their economies vanish. Following an assessment and analysis, it becomes clearer that there are more areas of collaboration than areas of conflict.

The greatest method for the SAARC nations to collaborate is through increasing intra-regional commerce by providing each other with facilities. In order to decrease trade imbalances among Indo-Bangladesh, India and Bangladesh could provide an example in considering establishing a bilateral free movement agreement and using southern Chittagong port as a transit for ferrying products to North-Eastern India. Indo-Sri Lanka may also boost many commodities, such as tea and rubber.

---

1. Ghosh, A and P Sen (2012) Privatisation in a Small Open Economy with Imperfect Competition, Journal of Public Economic Theory, 14, 3, 441-71

There are tremendous opportunities for growth among South Asian countries, and mutual collaboration is readily possible to expand telecommunications, roads, transportation, energy and other infrastructure amenities. The rail and road transit of India, Bangladesh and Pakistan, Nepal and Bhutan may easily be improved[1]. Furthermore, Bhutan and Nepal have potential for hydropower, which may simply be transported from India. Like river valley projects, Bhutan and Nepal may be developed in mutual interest and mutual advantage in flowing water between India and Bangladesh, India and Pakistan, Nepal and Bhutan. Furthermore, adequate water resources management, floods and droughts may be reduced to their agricultural advantage. In developing common telecommunications services, weather reports, worldwide price and product market fluctuations, the sharing of scientific knowledge and especially the spread of pests and illnesses may be helpful.

1.11 The Policy Measures to Promote Cooperation

The SAARC countries recommended fostering collaboration amongst the nations:

(i) Instead of relying on information supplied by developed nations to minimise the information gap, the information system must be created by the SAARC members themselves. The creation of information will enable exporters and importers to identify the demand and supply situation of different commodities in the area of the SAARC. This would be the initial precondition for future collaboration.

(ii) Complementarities are needed instead of rivalry today. Conscious efforts are required to create economic complementarities via reorientation of the region's economy. Again, market growth for goods of each other, a decrease in transportation costs and other concessions may go a long way.

(iii) Cooperation in payments and financial transactions are the only way to expand commerce. A strong network of banks and other financial institutions for liberal loans is also urgently needed.

(iv) Tariff and non-tariff obstacles should be reduced which would be beneficial in the promotion of trade relations. For such

1. Kaur P (2007) Growth Acceleration in India, Economic and Political Weekly, 42, 15, 1380-1386

concessions, the SAARC nations may conclude bilateral and multilateral agreements.

(v) Political and regional conflicts are normal. There is considerable demand for Indian products in Pakistan and Bangladesh; however, owing to political connections, many trafficking and unregistered trade are taking place over the border in these commodities.

India's fear of economic dominance should be alleviated. India has 77% of its population, 72% of its area, 78% of its G.D.P., 88% of its exports and 81% of its imports. India must be extremely cautious in dealing with the other partners in this respect.

Chapter - 2

India's Perception of SAARC

None can deny that the 20th century integrated the world as never before. Despite numerous cleavages, there is more cooperation among nations today than at any time in the past. As a major and significant nation of South and Southeast Asia, India's efforts towards regional integration are particularly of immense significance.

Indians have been trying to integrate Asian Countries for a long time. It was during the Indian struggle for freedom that closer cooperation with how Asians became one of the basic objectives of Indians. It was as early as 1920 that Gandhijee wrote of the growing solidarity of the Asian countries. In 1922, C.R. Das, President of the Indian National Congress, urged Indian participation in an Asian Federation, which he regarded as inevitable. The need for the Asian Federation was again stressed in the Congress session of 1926.

From the very beginning, India's foreign policy has been one of keeping alert from the big blocks of nations- rival blocks and being friendly to all countries and not becoming entangled in any alliances, military or other which might drag India into any possible conflict. In one of his speeches, Nehru said, "We are prepared to associate ourselves with other countries in a friendly way we are associated today in the United Nations with a great number of countries in the world. Anything else that we might do will naturally have to be something that does not go against our association with United Nations. Alliances usually involve military and other commitments, and they are more binding. Other forms of association [1]Which do not bind in this manner and help bring together nations for consolidation and, where necessary, cooperation is far more desirable.

1. Charter of the South Asian Association for Regional Cooperation

Nehru again said in 1945 in Kashmir: "Small states of the world tomorrow have no future in store, and they are sure to be reduced to the status of satellite states - I stand for a South Asian Federation of India, Iran, Iraq, Afghanistan and Burma.

Nehrujee, again in his first broadcast as head of the interim government in 1946, said: We are of Asia, and the peoples of Asia are nearer and closer to use than others. India is so situated that she is the pivot of western, southern and south-east Asia. In the past, her culture flowed to all these countries, and they came to her in many ways. Those contacts are being renewed, and the future is bound to see a closer union between India and South-East Asia on the one side and Afghanistan, Iran and the Arab world on the other. To the furtherance of that close association of free countries, we must devote ourselves.

In light of these speeches delivered by Nehrujee, it is clear that he strongly favoured friendly cooperation among fellow Asians. The Indians took several steps to ensure closer ties among the countries of South Asia.

The first significant step towards Asian integration was taken by India when the first Asian Relations Conference was convened in New Delhi. Nehru was the guiding spirit behind it. He set the conference's tone, and his speech's most important elements were: (1) The proclamation of Asia's arrival on the world scene; (2) The stress on the need for greater Asian unity, and The need for greater regional cooperation. Nehru also referred to the "widespread urge and an awareness that the time has come for us, peoples for Asia to meet together, to hold together and to advance together. Among the most specific suggestions by Nehru was "out of this Conference some permanent Asian institute for the study of common problems and to bring close relations will also emerge perhaps a school of Asian studies.' It was indeed an initial effort pitched at social, cultural and economic problems.[1]

It needs to add here that the same approach prompted him to convene the eighteen nation Conference on Indonesia in Delhi in January 1949. The conference registered a strong protest against the Netherlands' second police action in Indonesia. Nehru made an open appeal for regional integration. He said, "The free countries of Asia should begin to think of some more permanent arrangement than the conference for effective mutual

1. Gautam, Prada, RN, Formation of the Southern Asia Association for Regional Cooperation Federation of Critical Care Nurses, The World of Critical Care Nursing, Vol 12 Issue

consultations and concerted effort in the pursuit of common aims - and in a spirit of selfishness or hostility to any other nation or group of nations, but in order to strengthen and bring nearer fulfilment of the aims and ideas of the charter of United Nations. In this world of hatred, conflict and violence, let us endeavour to work jointly and in cooperation with others of goodwill to further the cause of peace and tolerance and freedom."'

It was during this period that the Afro-Asian group came into existence. India's attitude to the question of integration took a distinct shape after 1951 when the President of the Philippines announced his intention of convening an international conference to consider organising an anti-communist Association of South-East Asia along the lines of the North Atlanta Treaty. This was the beginning of India's differences in approach and perceptions of regional cooperation. Nehru opposed this more and wanted Asian countries to be kept out of the global ideological conflict. The problem with Philippine's initiative was that any regional effort would be anti-communist in nature. India stated that such alliances would retard the chance of reducing world tensions and that an anti-communist block by itself was no answer to Asia's problems.

India's approach to regional cooperation took a different turn. It desperately tried to prevent South and South East Asia from cold war politics. But things took a dangerous turn when America agreed to give military aid to Pakistan, thus upsetting the entire balance of power in the region and bringing the superpowers into the doorsteps of South Asia.

Nehru vehemently criticised it and stated: "It is clear that the approach of military pacts, like the Baghdad pact and SEATO, is wrong, a dangerous approach and a harmful approach. It sets the entire wrong tendency in motion and prevents the right tendencies from developing.

However, Nehru did not easily give up his "Asian Vision" and continued to work for peace. It needs to be mentioned here that differences between Nehru and other Asian leaders centred on the general tone of the conference.

During the course of the Conference, Nehru failed to prevent ideological cleavages simmering at the plenary sessions and to prevent discussion on specific bilateral issues. As a consequence, the Indian approach to regional cooperation took a different shape altogether and expressed its inability to hold another conference of this sort. This was rooted in the Indian logic that other nations of the region have had no propensity for a consensus or either foreign or domestic policies. Thus, the kind of Asian regional cooperation that Nehru had envisioned got a further setback in the wake of the Sino-Indian war of 1962. The Chinese blow awakened India to the realisation that real security came through inner strength, both economic and military. Nehru said," The basic factor in defence is the country's industrial growth, and all the armies in the world without an industrial background cannot function.

During the 1950s and 1960s[1] India laid more emphasis on its technical and industrial growth due to hard realities and political compulsions. It turned to the USSR and other countries for economic assistance to develop itself economically. In his welcome speech to the guests at Moscow, Nehru said: "We are convinced that it is not by military pacts and alliances and by the piling of armaments that world peace and security can be attained. We are in no camp and military alliance. The only camp we would like to be in is the camp of peace and goodwill which should increase as many countries as possible and which should be opposed to none. The only alliance, We seek is an alliance based on goodwill and cooperation. If peace is to be sought, it has to be by the methods of peace and the language of peace and goodwill.

India followed a bilateral approach in its relations with South and South East Asia countries. It was prepared to promote regionalism in mutually agreed areas but was against forging defence and security arrangements. It was during the 1970s that India acquired self-sufficiency to a great extent, both in matters of economic development and defence preparedness. By 1977, our country had the world's third-largest standing army, fifth-largest air force, and eighth-largest Navy.

In the wake of the breakdown of the Bretton woods system, all the developing countries felt the need to strengthen their economic base by forging cooperation. These factors motivated India to take the initiative to promote regional cooperation in South and South East Asia.

Our country gave top priority to the economic sphere for forging real cooperation among the South Asian countries, and it is due to its leading role that resulted in the birth of the Asian Development Bank in 1965. It also played a significant role in instituting the Asian Council of Ministers for economic cooperation within the ESCAP/ECAPE, which held its first meeting in

1. Hugar, Dr Jayaprakash G and Kannappanavar, B. U., Research Contributions of SAARC Countries in Social Science: A Bibliometric Study (April 2, 2021). Library Philosophy and Practice (e-journal). 4345, 2020

1967. India also extended its wholehearted support in regard to ongoing efforts that held its first meeting in 1967. India also joined the ongoing efforts which led to the Bangkok Agreement of 1975 aimed at liberalising intra-regional trade. Thus it is clear that India had played a leading role in the quest for building up economic cooperation among the developing countries.

In light of the aforesaid facts, it is clear that India's perception of regionalism in Asia has changed with the changing political and economic scenario. However, the basic approach to regional cooperation has remained static. India vehemently opposes the idea of forging regional security arrangements because it will invite extra-regional powers. Our country has emphasized economic cooperation to realise the objectives of South Asian cooperation. It took each step very cautiously and moved step by step without displaying any over-enthusiasm toward the whole concept of regionalism in South Asia, fearing that SAARC.[1] might not take the form of a political Union in the future. Hence, the bilateral and contentious issues were deliberately ignored, and collaboration was made the lynchpin of the regional organisation.

When the idea of regional cooperation was first coined, India showed its unwillingness due to its past experiences with regional pacts in Asia. India feared that sooner or later, SAARC might also meet some fate; besides, India itself had doubts about ganging up on the neighbours against it. On the other hand, India recognised the economic gains of cooperation. It also felt that basic economic activities in the region and some kind of mutual cooperation were a must. Viewed in the above perspective, the contents of Bangladesh's proposal, as circulated, were quite close to India's conception of regional cooperation. The proposal was confined to economic, scientific, technical and cultural fields. So India accepted the proposal hoping that economic cooperation would help remove political distrust.

Right from the beginning, India's approach to regional cooperation has been to promote collective self-reliance and alleviate poverty and backwardness through self-help. The institutional framework agreed upon when SAARC was launched in August 1983 could be regarded as the first pragmatic step in the right direction.

17 On the very question of institutional arrangements, India had favoured going slow on the whole issue. It never tried to get the secretariat

1. Dhaka Declaration (First Summit) of Heads of State or Government (Dhaka

stationed into its territory, though it had comparatively better infrastructural facilities, nor was there any desire to have an Indian appointed as the first SAARC secretary General. 1' It has always been her perception that without the inclusion of core areas of economic activity, no substantial progress could be made by SAARC and that it cannot attain meaningful concepts in its absence.

In the inaugural address to SAARC standing Committee in New Delhi in February 1984, P.V. Narsimha Rao, the then Indian Foreign Minister, observed.

Among the most important areas that offer fruitful cooperation are trade and industrial development; there is considerable scope for the expansion of trade among the region's countries. There are obvious advantages in increasing our purchases from neighbouring countries and reducing our dependence on countries outside the region for our essential requirements. There is considerable enthusiasm in the private sector for the promotion of industrial cooperation in South Asia.

Again in the Foreign Ministers' meeting at Dhaka in December 1985, the then external affairs Minister, B.R. Bhagat, observed:

The possibilities of cooperation in such sectors as trade, industry, energy and environment should be explored through technical study. The objective of such a study should be to find a way of tapping the region's vast potential derived from geographical continuity in the economics of the countries of the region.

But the idea was not accepted by other member countries, particularly Pakistan, on the ground that the industrially strong economy of India would overwhelm their less developed economy.

Keeping in view the sensitivities of member nations, India tried to demonstrate its accommodative attitude that was reflected in Rajiv Gandhi's speech at the Kathmandu Summit when he observed:

Now we are in a position to examine the extension of our cooperation to core economic sectors. It is true that the diversification of the economy is more pronounced in some member countries than in others. There are also directions and nuances in sovereign economic policies which must be respected. Some of these differences reflect not only incompatibilities but complementariness in our economies. None of these differences is fundamental. Regional approaches can be devised in the light of specific sensitivities and on the principle of unanimity.

After considerable assurance by India, the matter was given some consideration at the Kathmandu Summit, and finally, at the Islamabad Summit, it was agreed to call a meeting of planners of countries of the region to study the possibilities of cooperation in trade manufacturing and services.

Whereas on the one hand, the initiatives had finally been taken to include hardcore economic areas in the SAARC activities; on the other, the question of foreign funds appeared to be controversial. Should the SAARC seek foreign capital for development projects or depend on regional resources was a big question on which the seven-nation group appeared to be sharply divided. In 1986, for the first time, Bangladesh brought up the proposal. At the foreign Ministers' meeting in November 1987, while Bhutan and Bangladesh were at the forefront in pointing out the need for external assistance, other member countries except India supported the idea. The South Asian Region being a poor region and the mere contention that foreign assistance will help establish economic balance vis-â-vis India were some of the factors which helped for a ready approval by other countries.

As regards India has been opposing the idea of linking regional development to the availability of foreign funds. India had expressed doubts whether SAARC could raise capital from the commercial market whether SAARC could raise capital from the commercial market when international financial institutions themselves were suffering from a paucity of resources. Besides, India considered the proposal incompatible with the objective of self-reliance and self-dependency. Besides, India warned the member countries against the dangers of neo-colonialism, external pressure, etc. In his plea for retaining the economic independence of SAARC, Natwar Singh emphasised that at any cost, SAARC cannot be allowed to become adjunct to other means of mobilising foreign resources.

During the preparatory phase of the Foreign Ministers meeting of the Bangalore Summit, terrorism was a major issue. Though there was a general agreement among all member countries that concerted action must be taken against all forms of terrorism, India and Sri Lanka differed on the definition of terrorism. Sri Lanka was for ignoring the political and human rights aspects while making acts of terrorism extraditable. It wanted national focal points to be identified in the regional plan for fighting terrorism. It even submitted a test of offences for being regarded as a terrorist and not political for the purpose of extradition.

India took a long-term view and drew the attention of member-nations of the SAARC; to several international conventions related to terrorism that India had signed, like the Montreal, Tokyo and Hague conventions. However, in order to accommodate the political sensitivities of neighbouring regions, India declared that it was prepared to join other countries in taking follow-up action on the recommendation of the expert groups, which had suggested greater cooperation among law enforcement authorities. Finally, it was only under India's SAARC Chairmanship that the draft of the regional convention for the suppression of terrorism was finalised. It was later signed at the Kathmandu Summit.

India had all along favoured cooperation not only within the respective governments but among the people as well. However, the impediments at political and psychological levels had so far overlooked all the commonalities and severely hampered smooth communication between the people. It was with this view in mind that P.V. Narsimha Rao, the then Minister of External Affairs of India, in his speech at the foreign ministers meet at Male in July 1984, observed.[1]

For the process of Regional Cooperation to have maximum impact, it is necessary to ensure the participation not only of the governments but of the people themselves, including intellectuals, research scholars and representatives of private trade and industry.'

In his speech at the second Summit at Bangalore in November 1986, Prime Minister Rajiv Gandhi stressed this point again as the first step towards sound cooperation between the member countries. He said: "Regional cooperation cannot merely emerge from the fiats of leaders ...it is also through building a network of contacts at all levels among professionals among many disciplines that we can start giving real content to regional cooperation.'

The environmental dimension is also implicit in the objectives and programmes of SAARC, which envisages that its seven member countries would pool their resources of knowledge and expertise to benefit the region as a whole. South Asia as a whole may be viewed as one of the most calamities-ridden regions in the world, given the relentless sought of floods, droughts and landslides that occur regularly. Nineteen eighty-seven, of course, had been a particularly bad year. While India witnessed

1. K. Home, India's Evolving Approach to Regionalism: SAARC and Beyond, Rising Powers Quarterly Volume 2, Issue 3, 2017, 147-16.

the worst-ever drought in living memory, Bang\adesh and Nepal reeled under devastating floods, and the Maldives suffered heavy losses from tidal waves.

Recognising that these natural disasters are often symptoms of general environmental degradation in the South Asia region, the Kathmandu summit entrusted the secretary general to commission a study for analysing the causes and consequences of natural disasters and identifying ways and areas of protecting and preserving the environment. Rajiv Gandhi, in his speech at the Kathmandu Summit, observed the same when he stated:

> "the environment is an area where cooperation is indicated. Development and environment are interlinked. The degradation problem spills across natural frontiers, and conservation benefits spread across political boundaries. The development of each four economies is likely to be more sustained through regional cooperation, which preserves and improves the environment.

Bilateral versus 'regional' is a politically sensitive and long-standing question of debate in South Asian relations. It is also a fact that almost every bilateral controversy includes India as a party because it is only India which has common geographical, sociocultural and economic bounds with each of the South Asian countries. But it is unrealistic to attempt a regional solution to the specific bilateral problem such as the Kashmir issue between India and Pakistan, sharing of river waters between India and Bangladesh, the Tamil issue between India and Sri Lanka, the problem of trade and transit between India and Nepal etc. The smaller nations are busy discussing their bilateral problems within the SAARC forum to join a better bargaining deal vis-â-vis India without realising that it is against the spirit of the SAARC Charter. India's size, military, industrial, scientific and nuclear capabilities have caused consternation nation among smaller nations of the region.

On the contrary, India perceives its strength as a physical and psychological necessity to deter extra-regional threats to the security and stability of the region. In fact, ruling sections in New Delhi have been alarmed that India does not harbour any sinister designs against any other country of the sub-continent. They plead that India has never been a predatory state in the past, nor has it been an expansionist power to dominate others.

Then what should India do? How acclimate can trust be generated? The crucial test of India's leadership lies in restoring confidence in the South Asian Nations and shaping the regional framework. There is no gainsaying that the rule of intra-regional cooperation lies in India's equation with other South Asian states. Indeed without India's active participation, SAARC would be robbed of its very meaning.

On the other hand, one of the most important assumptions behind SAARC is the desire of India's neighbours for greater political and economic equity in a regional structure, which remains heavily weighted in favour of India. The combined resources and power potential of all the rest put together cannot equal that of India, conferring a certain centrality on India as a regional grouping of clearly unequal numbers. In the event, charges of India's high-handedness find a ready chord of response in the neighbourhood.

Today, when SAARC deliberations are stuck in the mire of unseemly procedural wrangles, uncertainty regarding the timing and venue of the next summit has brought into focus the fragile foundation on which SAARC rests. This had raised a big question mark on its future at a time when it was inching its way towards evolving a distinct regional identity. It must be pointed out that SAARC Summits have acquired a political significance beyond the SAARC framework. The question that must exercise all the countries of South Asia is whether any country, big or small, can be allowed to risk the collective interests of the region for their individual compulsions and priorities. On balance, the answer to that question would hold the key to the future of SAARC.

The main problem before our country is how we should behave with other Asian members. If India goes faster, the smaller nations may read some ulterior motives in the pace; if India sits back, it will deprive India of its historical role. If India stays on the sidelines, the SAARC may not attain its full status. The crucial question, therefore, remains: Can India strike a dynamic balance between enterprise and inaction, or for that matter, desirability and practicability with regard to regional cooperation in South Asia?

Despite the dilemma, one should hope that SAARC becomes a successful forum for cooperation among the region's member countries. Prime Minister Rajiv Gandhi aptly expressed India's aspirations in this regard in his address at the inaugural plenary of the SAARC Summit:

"Certainly, we have problems and difficulties, and these do impose constraints on us. Enduring cooperation is cooperation adapted to the realities of our condition. The model we have evolved for ourselves is a model which is in accord with our realities, our compulsions and our genius. We have not sought to melt our bilateral relations into a common regional identity but rather to fit south Asian cooperation into our respective foreign policies as an additional dimension. We have evolved modalities which do not allow bilateral strains to impinge on regional cooperation. Our cooperation tempers enthusiasm with pragmatism and initiative with consensus. At the same time, in the light of our experience, of the recent past, we have every reason to hope that the practice of regional cooperation will have a beneficial impact on bilateral relationships."

Two dominant forces have been shaping the world economy during the last quarter of the 20th century—globalisation and regionalisation. Regional economic integration has occurred simultaneously and is linked to the process of globalisation. The General Agreement on Tariffs and Trade (GATT), and its successor organisation World Trade Organization (WTO), have recognised the role of Regional Trade Agreements (RTAs) in the world economy. Multilateral trade liberalisation had led to an exponential growth of the world economy, benefiting many nations, yet it became clear from both North and South in Seattle and in other places that increasing trade openness was imposing a tremendous short-term cost to developing as well as some sectors of the developed countries. Regional cooperation is seen by the participating countries as a counter-availing power in trade negotiations with the countries outside the region, besides providing opportunities to benefit from trading with the neighbours.

Most of the newly liberated countries of Asia, Africa and Latin America have faced tremendous difficulties in planning their development strategies because of a number of potential problems like population explosion, lack of technology and skilled manpower, low rate of growth, poor per capita income, galloping inflation, unfavourable balance of trade and low productivity etc. Their problems are further accelerated due to the lack of cooperation by the developed countries. In spite of several rounds of North-South dialogues under the auspices of the United Nations Conference on Trade and Development (UNCTAD) and the United Nations Industrial Development Organization (UNIDO), one hardly notices any ray of hope for the developing countries. Major reforms in the world economy have been suggested by the well-known New International Economic

Order (NIEO) resolution of the U.N. General Assembly in 1974 and thereafter reemphasised from time to time in the final declarations of the Non-Aligned Summits and the meetings of the Commonwealth Heads of State or Government. But the developed nations have turned de fear to such suggestions.

With such a gloomy scenario regarding the outcome of the North-South Dialogue, several rounds of discussions have been initiated among the developing states for more meaningful interaction among themselves. Developing countries, including South Asia, face the precise role of regional cooperation in the rapidly globalising world. In view of the large gains from multilateral trade liberalisation, South Asia needs to continue on the trade liberalisation front; this does not stand in the way of enhanced regional cooperation.

World trade has grown at an average rate of 6 per cent over the past decade or so, at twice the growth rate of world GDP. On January 1, 1995, the WTO replaced GATT, which dealt only with trade in goods and included in its mandate to monitor and implement agreements on commodities, services, and intellectual property rights and a mechanism for dispute settlement. Now, with more countries becoming members of the WTO, the global trading order is what WTO rules make it to be. In 1999, more than two-thirds of the 140 members (as on November 30, 2000) of the WTO were developing countries with approximately a 20 per cent share of world exports. This has wide-ranging implications for the global economy.[1]

2.1 REGIONAL TRADING GROUPS:

Looking at the current trend in forming regional trading blocs, one can see that nearly all of the WTO's 140 members have notified participation in one or more Regional Trade Agreements (RTA's), customs unions, free trade areas or other preferential arrangements. In 1948-1994, the GATT received 124 notifications of RTA's (relating to trade in goods), and since the creation of the WTO, 90 additional arrangements covering trade in goods or services have been notified. Out of the total of 214 agreements and/or enlargements so far notified to the GATT/WTO,134 are deemed to be currently in force. The network of RTAs throughout the world is now highly complex, and many countries are members of several agreements, sometimes with very differing rules.

1. Jayawardena, R., Ranasinghe, P., Byrne, N.M. *et al.* Prevalence and trends of the diabetes epidemic in South Asia: a systematic review and meta-analysis. *BMC Public Health* 12.

The Mahbub UI Haq Human Development Centre, in its report, cited four motivating factors for forging regional alliances. These are

- To promote economic cooperation among the members of the group by increasing efficiency and exploiting economies of scale;
- To achieve international competitiveness during globalisation
- To build a sense of security and to facilitate political harmony within a region; and
- To forge a collective bargaining position in global negotiations.

During the last two decades of the 20th century, there was a great rush of regional alliances around the world. There is considerable debate over the nature and future of these regional alliances under the auspices of the WTO. As to their future role, it is not certain whether their recognition in the WTO framework, viz., Article XXIV, is to attract existing regional blocs to enter the WTO membership or merely to promote the existence of such regional (preferential) trading blocs as a complementary instrument to the working of WTO. Another view is that Article XXIV of the WTO may, at a later date, translate into phasing out mechanisms for these regional blocs. By examining the nature of these blocs, some insist on calling these alliances' preferential' rather than regional or free trade agreements.

2.2 SOUTH ASIA — ECONOMIC CONDITIONS

All the South Asian States fall in the category of less developed states of the Third World. All of them are faced with the challenges of low rate of economic growth, high rate of population growth, underutilisation of manpower resources, high incidence of poverty income inequalities, food shortage, adverse terms of trade, the heavy balance of payment deficits, high cost of oil imports, heavy debt service burdens, inflation and similarly other related problems. The SAARC countries are of different sizes and population-wise and have different factor endowments. They account for about 21 per cent of the world's population and 3.5percent of the total land areas, buttheirshareinworldoutputismere1.3percent Furthertheirshare in-world merchandise trade is about 1 per cent only. About half of the world's poor are found in these countries. The economic structure of these countries is basically agrarian, and about three-fourths of their total population subsists in agriculture. These similar conditions compelled the countries of the region to forge an alliance for economic development.

The economic backwardness of the region is so universal that except for the Maldives and Sri Lanka, the rest of the SAARC countries, i.e., India, Pakistan, Afghanistan, Bangladesh, Nepal and Bhutan, consisting of 98% of the total population of the region figure in the low Human Development Indexgroupof44 countries prepared by UNDP.

The economic system among the SAARC countries is the same as that of a mixed economy because of their under-development characteristics and adoption of the planning process for their development. These countries have various economic features in common, like poverty, dependence on agriculture, low productivity and mass unemployment; industrial backwardness further adds to the already existing underemployment and unemployment in this region. Industrial production accounts for about one-fourth of the gross domestic product and provides employment to less than 15 per cent of the total population of this region.

Keeping in view of these anomalies, South Asian countries came to a common platform for the speedy economic growth of the region. Recognising the value of regional cooperation in both economic and non-economic spheres and despite being confronted with some of the most intense political issues, the seven South Asian States formally launched the South Asian Association for Regional Cooperation (SAARC) on December 7 1985. SAARC is an institutional arrangement to encourage mutual cooperation among its member states.

Explaining the necessity of regional cooperation, particularly in the economic sphere, the 'Bangladesh Working Paper' pointed out, "the efforts have not fully exploited the vast potential of regional cooperation that exists and the consequential benefits that this will bring, collectively and individually, to the countries of the region. The collective economic benefit is the main rationale as well as the drive behind SAARC'. The Bangladesh proposal argued that inherent logic strongly justifies regional cooperation, particularly among South Asian countries, because the countries in the region enjoy geographical contiguity and historical, social, cultural and ethnic affinities, which would act as centripetal forces and, thus, contribute substantively to facilitate coordination and to reducing of transaction costs.

2.3 Economic Initiative before the Formation of SAARC

The Foreign Secretaries of the seven South Asian countries agreed at their first meeting in Colombo (21-23 April 1981) to pursue cooperation in five broad areas: agricultural, rural development, telecommunication, meteorology and health and population services. The Foreign Secretaries also agreed to set up a 'Committee of the Whole' comprising senior officials from the seven countries to identify and report on other areas of possible cooperation. Thus Committee, at its first meeting held in Colombo in August-September 1981, expressed the need to expand economic relations and the need for cooperation in international economic negotiations.

In 1983 (24-25 January), the first meeting of the representatives of 'The National Planning Organisation' was held in New Delhi. This was, in fact, the first 'economic' meeting at a regional level among South Asian countries. The meeting focused on three areas: national planning models and techniques, poverty alleviation programmes, and the global economic situation. The meeting agreed on the need for regular consultations and exchange of information, but more importantly, it called for the systematic exploration of the scope for intra-regional economic cooperation.

The main objectives laid down in the SAARC Charter adopted at the first summit are to promote the welfare of the peoples of South Asia; accelerate economic growth and social progress; promote active collaboration in the economic, social, cultural, technical and scientific fields; strengthen cooperation in international forums on matters of common interest, and cooperate with international and regional organisations with similar aims and purposes.

2.4 Economic Initiatives after the Formation of SAARC

After the declaration of the SAARC Charter, the first 'Ministerial Meeting on International Economic Issues' was held in Islamabad in March-April 1986. The declaration of this Ministerial Meeting stressed the need for intensifying economic cooperation among SAARC countries and also agreed that SAARC countries should coordinate their positions at the various headquarter of regional and international organisations as well as in relevant international conferences to further the common objectives of member countries.

The second meeting of the 'National Planning Organization' was held in Islamabad in October 1987. It recommended that in view of the region's adverse international economic situation, there was a need to pool resources for long-term regional cooperation. The representatives of the meeting felt the need to constitute a study group to identify priority areas for regional economic cooperation.

Accordingly, the first attempt made towards moving into core areas of trade and economic cooperation was the commissioning by the SAARC Secretariat, a regional study on 'Trade Manufacturers and Services (TMS). The TMS study was completed in 1991. It outlined a number of recommendations for promoting regional cooperation in the core economic areas.[15] It considered economic cooperation among the countries of the SAARC region as an inevitable imperative for promoting the all-around development of the region.

In May 1991, the Council of Ministers, at their Ninth session at Male, endorsed the study of the TMS and established a high-level committee known as the Committee on Economic Cooperation(CEC) comprising Commerce/Trade Secretaries of the SAARC Member States. The CEC was mandated to formulate and oversee the implementation of specific measures, policies and programmes within the SAARC framework to strengthen and enhance intra-regional cooperation in the field of trade and economic relations. With the creation of the CEC, regional economic cooperation was formally institutionalised. Their commendations of the CEC are submitted to the Standing Committees of Foreign Secretaries and through it to higher bodies, namely the Council of Ministers and the Summit.

At its third meeting in New Delhi in November 1991, the CEC recommended that the Draft Agreement on SAARC Preferential Trade Agreement (hereafter SAPTA) with few modifications be approved by the Council of Ministers at its next Twelfth Session in Dhaka.17 In December 1991, the Sixth Summit, held in Colombo, approved the establishment of an inter Governmental Group' (IGG) to formulate an agreement to establish a SAARC Preferential Trading Agreement (SAPTA) by1997.

2.5 SAPTA

Given the consensus within SAARC, the Council of Ministers signed the Framework Agreement on SAPTA in Dhaka on April 11 1993. The signing of SAPTA was a landmark achievement for South Asian countries. The New Delhi Summit held from 2^n to May 4 1995, formally approved the proposals for preferential trade worked out by the Inter-Governmental Group (IGG) and later endorsed by the SAARC Foreign Ministers with all the member countries ratified the agreement; the same came into force on December 7 1995-the date which marks the end of the first decade of SAARC's experience.'

2.5.1 Salient Features of the SAPTA Agreement

The operationalisation of the SAPTA Agreement is the real beginning of SAARC. This agreement is recognised as the first step towards a higher level of regional trade and economic cooperation. It aims[1]to promote and sustain mutual trade and economic cooperation among the member countries through exchanging concessions. It promotes intra-SAARC trade through a reduction in tariffs, para-tariffs, and non-tariff measures and taking direct trade measures like buy-back arrangements, state trade operations, etc. Member countries agreed to undertake appropriate steps and measures for developing and improving the communication system, transport infrastructure and transit facilities to accelerate the growth of trade.

2.5.2 Principles of SAPTA:

The following principles of SAPTA

1. SAPTA shall be based and applied on the principles of overall reciprocity and mutuality of advantages in such a way as to benefit equitably all Contracting States taking into account their respective levels of economic and industrial development, the pattern of their external trade, trade and tariff policies and systems;
2. SAPTA shall be negotiated step by step, improved and extended in successive stages with periodic views;
3. The special needs of the Least Developed Contracting States shall be clearly recognised, and concrete preferential measures in their favour should be agreed upon;
4. SAPTA shall include all products, manufactures, and commodities in their raw, semi-processed and processed

2.6 Intra-Regional Trade

The SAARC countries are highly dependent on the world's advanced countries for their trade relations. Though the importance of the developing countries has grown significantly for their mutual trade among themselves, the SAARC trade relations have been strongly linked with the developed world. Historically, the trade relations among SAARC countries have been

1. Jayawardena, R., Ranasinghe, P., Byrne, N.M. *et al.* Prevalence and trends of the diabetes epidemic in South Asia: a systematic review and meta-analysis. *BMC Public Health* 12.

continuously at a low level. The bulk of their exports and imports have largely with the developed countries. Further, the terms of trade of these countries have become unfavourable due to their low export prices and high import prices. Their export products face tough competition in the world market because of their high cost compared to developed countries products. Thus these countries are facing continuously unfavourable balance of trade with the rest of the world.

The share of SAARC countries in the World Trade depicts a rather discouraging picture. Their share in the world exports and imports was 7.2 and 5.3 per cent, respectively, in 1938. The respective share declined to 0.99 per cent and 0.94 per cent in 1972. During 1975- 91 the share of SAARC in the world exports and imports remained at 0.80 per cent and 1.19 per cent in world exports and imports, respectively, on an average per annum. The share of SAARC in the total trade turnover of the world during 1995 was 1.05percent only.

SAPTA was envisaged primarily as the first step towards the transition to a South Asian Free Trade Area (SAFTA), leading subsequently towards Customs Union, Common Market and Economic Union. In the Eighth SAARC Summit held in New Delhi in May 1995, India proposed the transition from SAPTA to SAFTA. In the sixteenth session of the Council of Ministers held in New Delhi on 18- 19th December 1995, it agreed on the meet to strive for the realisation of SAFTA. To this end, an Inter-Governmental Expert Group (IGEG) was set up in 1996 to identify the necessary steps towards moving into a free trade area.

2.6.1 SAARC Economic Cooperation Conference

The SAARC Chamber of Commerce and Industry (SCCI) and the Federation of Indian Chamber of Commerce and Industry (FICCI) organised an economic Cooperation Conference on November 19, 1996., While inaugurating the SAARC Economic Cooperation Conference, the then-Indian Prime Minister Sri. H.D. Deve Gowda underscored the need for regional agreement of conventions on investment promotion and protection, avoidance of double taxation, customs harmonisation and cooperation among the SAARC countries. The delegates felt that the trade liberalisation had gotten the right impetus in the SAARC region. It also opined that consensuson1200 it is essential to keep open for tariff reduction among SAARC nations. 2 Such a step goes a long way in further ensuring the implementation of SAFTA.

2.6.2 Economic Cooperation Conference (ECC)

Indian Chamber of Commerce oorganised ECC on December 20, 1996, at Calcutta. Members of the Federation of Pakistan Chan of Commerce and Industry (FPCC) expressed eagerness to increase trade and business exchanges with India. Pakistan was prepared to exchange engineering goods for Indian Tea on a barter basis. In the meeting, delegates from Dhaka requested for removal of tariffs on 210 items, and India conveniently agreed to waive customs duty on 164 items.

2.6.3 SAARC Council of Ministers Meeting

The then-Indian Prime Minister Sri inaugurated the 17th session of the SAARC Council of Ministers. H.D. Deve Gowda on December 19, 1996. In his address, he vehemently suggested that efforts be made to make the South Asian Free Trade Area (SAFTA) the early deadline for which was the year 2000 and the latest 2005 - operational in 1998. He remarked, 'The SAFTA will make the regional grouping a strong economic entity.26 The formation of SAFTA (at an early stage) would help remove trade barriers and possibly enable the member-states to overcome the contentions on bilateral issues. It is felt that SAFTA's inception could also result in extending of concession of tariffs and favourable treatment to the Least Developed Countries (LDCs) in the region.

Recognising the need to address asymmetries in development and other complexities that may stand in the way of such a tight schedule, the Tenth Colombo Summit directed that the text of the regulatory framework for creating a Free Trade Area in the region should be finalised. In this connection, a Committee of Experts has been constituted to draft a comprehensive treaty which, following its first meeting in Kathmandu (July 1999), worked out its broad terms of reference. Eventually, the treaty would incorporate, inter alia, binding time frames for freeing trade measures to facilitate trade and protection of LDC, including mechanisms for compensation of revenue loss etc.27 after setting the Committee of Experts, the Inter-Governmental Export Group (IGEG) was winded up.

All the member countries of SAARC have shown keen interest in the Ninth SAARC Summit held in Male in May 1997 to advance the deadline for the implementation of SAFTA from 2005 to 2001. India's proposal for the SAARC Economic Community (SAEC) after attaining the goal of SAFTA also responded positively at this summit. However, the targets could not be met, and it was decided at the Eleventh Summit held at

Kathmandu from 4th to 6h January, decided that the goal should be attained by the end of 2002.[1]

2.7 SAFTA

The Twelfth SAARC Summit scheduled in 2003 was delayed due to escalating tensions between India and Pakistan. So the issue of the SAFTA agreement was also delayed. However, the Twelfth SAARC Summit was held in 2004 in Islamabad. The one success that had been eluding the SAARC Summit for quite some time and keeping the member states at loggerheads with each other has ultimately been accomplished. The Islamabad Summit of SAARC has produced a fine blueprint for the region's future economic development and integration in the form of a masterpiece known by the nomenclature of SAFTA. The agreement signed at the 12th SAARC Summit is a huge morale booster for the region. The SAFTA agreement was signed by the Council of Ministers of the region in 2004, and the summit formally approved it.

2.7.1 Salient Features of SAFTA

The SAFTA, signed on January 6 2004, has the following features:.'

- The objective of the agreement was to promote and enhance mutual trade and economic cooperation by eliminating barriers of the trade-in and facilitating the cross-border movement of goods between the territories of the region.
- It suggested fair competition in the free trade area and ensured equitable benefits to all members of the region.
- It is decided to create an effective mechanism for the implementation of the agreement and resolving disputes.
- It involves the free movement of goods between countries through inter-alia, the elimination of tariffs, para tariffs and non-tariff restrictions on the movement of goods.
- Keeping in view the special needs of the Least Developed Countries, it adopts concrete preferential measures in their favour on a non-reciprocal basis.

1. Das JK, Rizvi A, Bhatti Z, Paul V, Bahl R, Shahidullah M, Manandhar D, Stanekzai H, Amarasena S, Bhutta ZA. State of neonatal health care in eight countries of the SAARC region, South Asia: how can we make a difference? Paediatr Int Child Health. 2015.

- For mutual benefit, it decided to simplify and harmonisation the customs clearance procedure.

It was decided that the agreement shall enter into force on January 1 2006, upon completion of formalities, including ratification by all contracting States and issuance of notification thereof by the SAARC Secretariat. This agreement shall supersede the agreement of SAPTA.

2.7.2 Superiority of SAFTA over SAPTA

SAFTA has more chances of success than SAPTA due to the fact that the former may encourage greater cooperation in areas such as investments and the formation of a common energy grid. Bhutan and Nepal have surplus power, and there could be the import of energy into India. But the possibility of having a quantum jump in trade in goods is not very encouraging. It is not expected to lead to any immediate jump in exports to India since as many as 884 specific product groups have been kept on the sensitive list where the trade liberalisation programme would not be applicable. Other countries in the SAARC region had a limited trade basket mainly comprising textiles and plantation sector items, whereas India's sensitive list includes goods mainly from the agriculture sector, textiles, chemicals and leather and those reserved for the small-scale sector. SAFTA would encourage more textile trade between India and the LDC so far SAARC, and the same could not be said about the plantation sector. As most of the items under the plantation sector are kept on the sensitive list, there is limited scope for trade enlargement in this area. SAFTA deal is likely to work in favour of LDCs such as Bangladesh, which is already a low-cost manufacturer of textiles and would get preferential access to the huge Indian market.'

The two select features of SAFTA—the rules of origin and the sensitive list — demonstrate everything. Three areas were clearly identified in SAFTA at the 13th summit. (i) negative lists dealing with the exclusion of commodities not falling within the consist of free trade;(ii) the rules of origin to ensure that third country goods did not slip into intra-regional trade without adequate value addition in a member-nation; and (iii) the rescue composition of LDCs to compensate than for the loss of duties following free trade. SAFTA is heavily skewed in favour of the LDCs, not merely on the staggered tariff reduction schedule but also in the drawing up of the negative lists of items not covered by the agreement. Effective implementation of SAFTA will determine the larger success of SAARC.

The process of integration of economies of the SAARC members has been painfully slow. Four countries remain in the LDC category, and two or three of them have moved to a much higher level of growth and development. More important political differences have made the grouping random all the years. Because of the undue delay in implementing SAFTA, India signed a bilateral FTA with Sri Lanka in the region and a few others. Implementing SAFTA is going to be two stage process—India, Pakistan, and Sri Lanka are to bring their tariffs in line in 2013, and the rest of the region will follow suit by 2018.

The new regime can succeed only through a process of consensus and compromise; trade is a two-way street. Suppose India opened up to its neighbours, allowing them to enter the domestic market. In that case, they might be liberal in opening up their marketplace, and ultimately price and quality would settle the demand-supply equations. It is said that India had bowed to the domestic industries and has not played much to the expectations in proportion to the size of India's economy and its diversified nature. It is a known fact that developing countries pay as much as 70% of tariffs, and that is why Asian countries have started helping their poor by lowering regional tariffs on key products. But it is not taking place in SAARC, where India is the leader cruising on a high growth strategy with foreign exchange reserves running at 140 billion dollars.

2.7.3 SAARC Trade Fairs

The holding of SAARC Trade Fairs has become a regular feature since 1996 when the first SAARC Trade Fair was held in New Delhi in January 1996 with the theme "Cooperation for Growth". The Fair, organised as a part of the commemoration of the first decade of SAARC, was jointly inaugurated by the Commerce Ministers and leaders of delegations of Member States. The Fair provided a befitting venue for the representatives of the business and industry of SAARC member countries to discuss various issues connected with the promotion and expansion of intra-SAARC trade. The Trade Fairs have succeeded in projecting the region's potential and promoting the wide variety of products the region produces, which match international quality and standards. The SAARC Secretariat has also set up stalls at Trade Fairs to inform the public of SAARC activities.[1]

---

1. Keshab Raj Bhattarai, 2016. "Economic Growth and Development in India and SAARC Countries," EcoMod2016 9631

2.7.4 Dominating Partner: India

One of the South Asian region's basic features is India's compelling presence, with a gigantic size in terms of population, area and economy. India shares three-fourths of the economy of entire South Asia. This is both a source of strength and also creates certain discomforts for India as it overcomes smaller neighbours, though India's per capita income and foreign trade as a percentage of GNP are lower than most of the SAARC member countries.

India is an agriculture-based country sharing nearly 31 per cent of the GDP in 2001. While the industry share is 30 per cent, the manufacturing sector alone contributed nearly 20 per cent in 2001. The analysis of the share of GDP exhibit that the share of agriculture is decreasing; This indicates that the country is shifting to a developing and industrial economy. The country's per capita income was estimated at US 2230 Dollars in 2001, and the real growth rate estimated for the last decade, 1999-2000, was 3.5 per cent. But the real growth rate during the period 2000-2001 was only 2.9 per cent. This was because of the adverse impact of the Gulf crisis.

2.7.5 Travel of India's Trade with SAARC

Generally, the foreign trade of a country includes exports and imports. The following are the important items of exports and imports from India to SAARC countries and from SAARC states to India.

- **Afghanistan:**

  India signed a Preferential Trade Agreement (PTA) on March 6, 2003, with Afghanistan, according to which the Government of Afghanistan grants preferential tariffs on eight items exported from India, including Tea, medicines, sugar, and cement. The other major exports to Afghanistan from India include articles of iron or steel, clothing accessories, aluminium articles, electrical machinery, nuclear reactors and boilers etc. The major imports from Afghanistan include goods like edible oil, fruits and nuts, gums, resins, carpets, paper and paper board etc.

- **Bangladesh:**

  The main components of India's exports to Bangladesh were cotton yarn, machinery and instruments, fruits and vegetables, spices, manmade yarn, fabrics and made-up drugs, pharmaceuticals and fine chemicals, rubber manufactured products, and transport equipment. The major imports from Bangladesh are News Print, Organic Chemicals, ores, metals crap, textile yarn and fabrics, transport equipment, non-ferrous metals, pearls, and precious and semi-precious stones. It is important to note that none of these items had a significant share in the imports from that country.

It is evident the percentage of share of India's exports to Bangladesh started declining gradually in 2004-2005, and in 2007-2008, a negative growth rate was registered in exports. While in the case of imports, the percentage of the share is not evenly distributed. The negative growth rate in imports was registered in 2004-2005. Unlike Afghanistan, the share of India's exports to Bangladesh reached nearly a per cent.

- **Bhutan:**

The Free Trade Agreement between India and Bhutan provides free trade between the two countries. Under this Agreement, India also provides shipment facilities through Indian Territory for Bhutan's trade with third countries. All the export transactions are carried out in Indian Rupees and Bhutanese Ngultrums.

The main components of India's exports to Bhutan are transport equipment, primary and semi-finished iron and steel, machinery and instruments, and manufacturers of metals, Tea, ores and minerals. The chief items of import are wood and wood products, Inorganic Chemicals, coal, coke and briquettes.

- **India's Trade with the Maldives:**

Trade between India and Maldives is governed by the rules mentioned in the Indo-Maldives Trade Agreement signed on March 31 1981. Under this agreement, Indian major export items to the Maldives include rice other than basmati, sugar, fresh vegetables, miscellaneous processed items, drugs, pharmaceuticals and fine chemicals, plastic and linoleum products, and manufacturers of metals and machinery equipment. The imports from the Maldives are insignificant; India and Maldives also share the status of most favoured Nations with each other.[1]

- **Nepal:**

Indo-Nepal Trade Treaty between India and Nepal is signed five

1. Russell, Hasibul & Kouraklis, John. (2017). Impact of Foreign Direct Investment on Economic Growth of the SAARC Countries.

years. Under this trade agreement, major items exported from India include drugs, pharmaceuticals and fine chemicals, petroleum products, pulses, transport equipment, rice other than basmati, tobacco manufacturers' spices, fresh fruits and vegetables, miscellaneous processed items, ores and minerals, glassware/ ceramics, manufacturers of metals, primary and semi- furnished iron and steel and cotton yarn fabrics etc. The major import from Nepal includes vegetable oil, cereal preparations, crude materials, wood and wood products, sugar and cereals.

- **India's Trade with Pakistan:**

  No trade agreement was signed between India and Pakistan till 2007. Although India has granted Pakistan the status of 'Most favoured Nation' since 1996, Pakistan has yet to reciprocate by granting this status to India. Indian exports to Pakistan are restricted to a list of 773items known as the positive list. Iron ore is the major export to Pakistan. Other exports were oil meals, dyes, tar and chemicals, spices, paint, enamel and varnish, ores and minerals, drugs, pharmaceuticals and fine chemicals, machinery and instruments. The chief components of imports include fruits, textile yarn, fabrics and made-ups, Meta lifers, ores and metal scrap, crude minerals, wood pearls and semi-precious stones.

- **India's Trade with Sri Lanka:**

  After Bangladesh, Sri Lanka is the biggest export market for India; Trade between the two countries is carried out as per guidelines mentioned in the Indo-Sri Lanka Free Trade Agreement. Major items of export from India have been pulses, wheat, other cereal spices, oil meals, fresh vegetables, miscellaneous processed items, drugs, pharmaceuticals and fine chemicals, inorganic/ organic agrochemicals, rubber, manufactured goods except for footwear, glass, glassware/chemicals and allied products, paper/ wood products, plastic and linoleum products, non-ferrous metals, manufacturers of metals, machinery and instruments, iron and steel bar/rod etc. Primary and semi-finished iron and steel, electronic goods, cotton yarn, fabric made-ups, and crude petroleum products. The largest components of India's imports from Sri Lanka are meta lifers, ores, metal scraps, manufacturers of metals, pulp and waste paper, and synthetic and reclaimed rubber.

Chapter

India's Bilateral Rel[illegible]

SAARC

Chapter - 3

India's Bilateral Relations with the SAARC Countries

One of the striking and peculiar features of South Asian states is the disparity in their size and their political, economic and military strengths and capabilities. There are small and sparsely populated states like Maldives and Bhutan and huge ones like Bangladesh, Pakistan and India. But when the comparison is made between South Asian states, India beats all other states. It is because India is the largest and strongest in terms of its area, political stability, economic viability and military capabilities. Thus India is termed the core state, while the other states are called the periphery of the South Asian regional system.

The size and strength of India are not only a source of embarrassment for India but also a cause of centrifugal tendencies in South Asia. The unenviable position of India emanates from the fact that India is the only state which shares territorial or maritime boundaries with almost all the States except the Maldives in the region.

The British exit in 1947 did two significant developments for South Asia. First, the British Raj withdrew from South Asia very haphazardly. They left things indecisive and incredibly territorial demarcation. India-Pak and India-China boundaries were not historically defined, which lately triggered territorial tensions. Secondly, the power status of India in 1947 made the South Asia balance of power revolve around it. The other countries of the region, like Pakistan, Nepal, Bangladesh, Bhutan and Sri Lanka, had individually and separately moved in common with India each other. Conversely, there is a bit of India in every other country of South

Asia. There was hardly anything significant and common between India's neighbours, and only India was common among them.[1]

The South Asian region had become Indo-centric geographically and in terms of socio-cultural continuities and economic infrastructure. Jawaharlal Nehru, the first Prime Minister of India, also pointed out the Indo-centric character of South Asia. He said that India is so placed in the South Asian region that whenever any problem arises, whether it is a problem of defence or trade or industry or economic policy. India always comes into the picture and cannot be ignored at all.

3.1 India's Geographical Position

India is a subcontinent stretching from the Himalayas to the Indian Ocean. It has the second-largest population and the seventh-largest territory in the world. India constitutes about 75 per cent of South Asia in demography, environment, and natural resources. It is the only state in the region whose boundaries has touched by land or water by all the other six states of South Asia. Four States felt India's boundaries by common land borders, e.g. Pakistan, Nepal, Bhutan, and Bangladesh. And the other two, i.e. Sri Lanka and the Maldives, touched India through common Maritime borders.

India's geographical position also makes it a powerful country among South Asian countries. Another reason for India's powerful status has been highlighted in the hierarchical power structure of the South Asian region. India and Pakistan were the powerful states of the South Asian region. Still, the breakup of Pakistan enhanced India's position within the area and made the system hierarchical regarding relative levels of power. Cohen park wrote, "A state such as India, by its size, resources and geographical location, finds itself a significant influence in regional terms, whether it seeks or not that label.

3.2 India's Relations with its Neighbours

The relationship is marked by suspicion, unfriendly postures and, at times, conflict. The actions and attitudes of all South Asian states except India were determined by India's actions and attitudes and small state tendencies. The South Asian relations are, thus, fitted into an action and

1. Paul, Aditi. (2020). Regional Cooperation in South Asia: Exploring the Three Pillars of Regionalism and their Relevance. The Journal of Indian and Asian Studies. 01. 2050008

reaction scenario; one may find an apparent lack of coordination and cooperation among these states in any meaningful sense. The Indo-centric nature of the region is also responsible for inter-state rivalry. Sri Lanka holds India accountable for Tamil militancy (now somehow ended). Pakistan desires Kashmir, and India questions its claim. Bangladesh harps upon the overwhelming size of India and holds it responsible for Chakma problems and water disputes. Nepal blames for Maoist insurgency and takes the side of China. Bhutan is worried about Nepal's demographic domination in its Southern part. Besides all this, India also has a sense of losing its territory because of China's claims.

South Asia is dominated by the actions and reactions by and against India. There is no denying that India is more than twice the other SAARC countries put together in size and nearly four times larger demographically than all the other South Asian Countries (SAARC Members) put together. Modern States enjoy political, economic and defence capabilities based on their size and resources. This strength indeed enjoys such status and power, but not to the disadvantage of any other state in its neighbourhood or in any other part of the globe. India's foreign policy objectives and postures also indicate this fact.

It cannot deny that India, to some extent, inherited the security perceptions of the previous British rulers. But India's foreign policy was inspired and cherished by the ideals and traditions of Indian political and cultural heritage and shaped by the mature vision of its first Prime Minister, Jawaharlal Nehru, who aimed at evolving friendly relations with its neighbours based on peace, mutual trust and cooperation. In this direction, it tried to lead the newly independent states of Asia and Africa with a fair measure of success. Unfortunately, its attention was drawn by India in various international forums and the vital Place it occupies in the United Nations, coupled with some of its actions in response to the regional crises in the past.

'Gujral Doctrine' as a catalyst on the road to cooperation

India's search for a cooperative neighbourhood and a peaceful and secure South Asia continued with a renewed emphasis when during a short period of 1996 97 Inder Kumar Gujral became the Foreign Minister and later Prime Minister of India. He advanced a principle known as the 'Gujral Doctrine', which envisaged an approach to resolving disputes and improving relations with neighbouring countries. It has two main elements

– (a) India's non reciprocal relations with its neighbours, (b) the Look East policy. Take up the entire Asia together. This initiative and push for peace in the region, with a history of hostility and mistrust, was probably encouraged by a decline in the fear of 'big India' among its neighbours in the changed international situation. The policy prescriptions of India in terms of Gujral doctrine were:

(a) Acknowledging its greater strength and larger size, India will be accommodating and generous towards her neighbours unilaterally to the maximum possible extent without demanding reciprocity;
(b) India will react to both internal and external developments in its neighbourhood from a moral high ground.'
(c) India will not allow its territory to be used against the interest of any country in the region;
(d) India will not interfere in the internal affairs of other countries in the area and would expect the others to observe this principle as well;
(e) India respects the territorial integrity and national sovereignty of all the states of the region,
(f) India is determined to settle all its disputes through peaceful bilateral negotiations.

Former Prime Minister, Gujaral maintained that implementing these principles would generate a climate of close and mutually benign cooperation in the region where the weight and size of India was regarded positively as an asset by these countries. The components of the Gujaral Doctrine were nothing new except the novelty of the principle of non-reciprocity. This principle, however, was presumably to be confined to the smaller neighbours - Bhutan, Bangladesh, Nepal and Sri Lanka. 'The non-reciprocity also meant that solution to one bilateral problem would not be linked to concessions by the other country for India on an issue that the latter considered beneficial.

However, The Current Prime Minister Narendra Modi's invitation to SAARC leaders for the inauguration ceremony and a bilateral meeting with each leader was unprecedented. This move emphasised the importance of SAARC for regional cooperation and showed India as the big brother of the group. It should be noted that India is not without bilateral problems with its neighbours. Neighbouring countries have issues related to conflict and mutual interests, and it is necessary to know the key areas of bilateral relations.

India has good bilateral relations with Afghanistan, Bangladesh, Bhutan, Maldives, Nepal and Sri Lanka. Per our 'Neighbourhood First' policy, India is an active development partner, and we are working on several projects in these countries. Interaction with these countries is based on a consultative, non-reciprocal and result-oriented approach to improve communication, improve infrastructure, and increase development cooperation in various fields, security and extensive people-to-people exchanges.

3.2.1 India and Afghanistan Relations:

India and Afghanistan have strong relations based on historical and cultural ties. The relationship has its foundations in historic contacts and exchanges between people. The friendly relations can be traced back to January 1950, when a five-year friendship treaty was signed by the then Prime Minister of India, Jawaharlal Nehru, and the then Afghan Ambassador to India, Mohammad Najibullah. Afghans supported Indians during the freedom struggle; contribution by Khan Abdul Gaffar Khan, revered as Frontier Gandhi;[1] India was the only South Asian country to recognise the Soviet-backed Democratic Republic of Afghanistan in the 1980s, and relations were weakened during the 1990s Afghan civil war and Taliban rule. India helped overthrow the Taliban and became Afghanistan's most significant regional provider of humanitarian and reconstruction aid.

Due to its geographical proximity and historical ties, India is a natural trading partner for Afghanistan and South Asia's largest market for its products. The total trade value between India and Afghanistan in CY 2019-2020 was $1.5 billion.[2] Salma Dam, officially the Afghanistan-India Friendship Dam, is a hydroelectric and irrigation dam project on the Hari River in the Chishti Sharif District of Herat Province in western Afghanistan. To strengthen relations between the two countries, the Afghan cabinet renamed the Salma Dam the Afghanistan-India Friendship Dam.

1. Ashraf, Fahmida. "INDIA-AFGHANISTAN RELATIONS: POST-9/11." Strategic Studies, vol. 27, no. 2, 2007, pp. 90–102. JSTOR, http://www.jstor.org/stable/45242397. Accessed 7 Oct. 2022.
2. Embassy of India, Kabul, Afghanistan, 'India-Afghanistan Relations' Online Retrieved From: https://eoi.gov.in/kabul/?0354?000

Another key initiative that has boosted bilateral trade was the opening of Chabahar Port in December 2017, followed by the signing of a trade agreement in February 2018 to manage port operations. Pulse was sent from India as an aid to Afghanistan via Chabahar. These were delivered to different regions of Afghanistan with an average transit time (excluding processing time) of less than two weeks. In 2019, Afghanistan sent about 700 tons of agricultural and mineral products to India through the Chabahar port.[1]. This clearly shows the feasibility of Chabahar port as a transit point to Afghanistan and, eventually, Central Asia. Afghanistan is of strategic importance to India as New Delhi seeks friendly allies in its neighborhood and because it is the gateway to energy-rich Central Asian countries such as Turkmenistan and Kazakhstan.

To combat the global pandemic of COVID-19 and related food security issues, India will deliver 75,000 MT of Wheat to Afghanistan in 2020. In addition, India has also undertaken a supply of 5 lakh tablets of Hydroxy-chloroquine, 1 Lakh tablets of Paracetamol and 50,000 pairs of surgical gloves to the Government of Afghanistan in 2020.[2]

However, despite being knocked off its feet by the collapse of the Ghani government of Afghanistan in mid-August 2021, New Delhi has quickly re-established its presence in the new Taliban-led Afghanistan. India moved quickly to assert itself as a significant stakeholder in Afghanistan after the fall of the Ghani government. At the same time, India gives off the impression it is playing a lone hand, it is acting in close coordination with the United States based on shared interests. Both nations seek to stabilise the country, promote an inclusive government and deny space to militant groups.[3] India has many reasons to foster closer relations with Afghanistan. Its policy is driven primarily by fears that a Taliban-run Afghanistan would enhance Pakistan's geopolitical heft. The Taliban is not seen as a threat to India, but its ties with Pakistan and jihadi groups such as Lashkar-e-Tayyiba and Jaish-e-Mohammad are worrisome. Afghanistan is crucial to India's continental economic

1. Embassy of India, Kabul, Afghanistan, 'India-Afghanistan Relations' Online Retrieved From: https://eoi.gov.in/kabul/?0354?000
2. Gupta Ashis, 'AFGHANISTAN AND INDIA'S FOREIGN POLICY', International Council for World Affairs, Online Retrieved From: https://www.icwa.co.in/afghanistan-and-indias-foreign-policy/
3. Joshi Manoj. (2022),' India's cautious return to Afghanistan,' Observer Research Foundation, Online Retrieved From: https://www.orfonline.org/research/indias-cautious-return-to-afghanistan/

aspirations, including closer ties with Central Asia and Iran, and Pakistan's blockade of Indian access to the region is currently hampered these goals.

In November 2021, India's National Security Advisor Ajit Doval hosted the Third Regional Security Dialogue on Afghanistan in New Delhi. India made it clear that its aim was not to resurrect an alliance to overthrow the Taliban but that it sought to prevent the revival of outfits like ISIS-K and Al Qaeda. This theme of non-interference in Afghanistan's internal affairs was repeated in the June 2022 talks. [1]

New Delhi has expressed its intention to strengthen relations with Kabul in a coordinated manner. A significant challenge for India is to address Pakistan's concerns that its presence in Afghanistan poses a security threat. In the past, Islamabad has used its agents to attack Indian targets, including the Indian embassy in Kabul. That's why India's first and foremost concern about Afghanistan is to ensure that Pakistan does not dominate the Afghan government structure. India feels that if Pakistan manages to establish a Taliban or Taliban-backed regime in Afghanistan, it will be detrimental to India's regional security. A stable Afghanistan bordering India is of vital importance for regional and national security and stability in South Asia and India. Afghanistan is significant as a tool against Pakistan and China.

3.2.2 Indo-Bangladesh Relations

The two neighbours, India and Bangladesh, are organically linked by a common heritage and shared history, shared memory of tragic loss and separation of large families after the partition of India in 1947. And both continue to expand bilateral relations between two countries. The geographical proximity of the two countries provides an opportunity for them to strengthen their communication and economy further. Before the partition of the Indian subcontinent in 1947, trade and commerce between the northeastern region of India and the rest of India was conducted through present-day Bangladesh.

Bangladesh shares a land border with India on three sides, and one side is along the Bay of Bengal. India and Bangladesh share 4096.7 km, and it is the longest land border shared by India with its neighbours. India was the first country to recognise Bangladesh as an independent and independent country and established diplomatic relations with the country as a friendly South Asian neighbor soon after its independence in December 1971.

1. Ibid.

Bangladesh plays a vital role in India's Neighborhood First Policy. The ties between India and Bangladesh are civilisational, cultural, social and economic. In 1972, India and Bangladesh signed the Treaty of Friendship and Cooperation, which laid the foundation for modern India-Bangladesh relations.[1]

India's geographical proximity to Bangladesh has made it one of its largest trading partners, and Bangladesh is India's sixth-largest trading partner. Since 2011, India has provided duty-free access to Bangladesh on all tariff items except tobacco and alcohol under the South Asian Free Trade Area (SAFTA).[2] Bilateral trade between the two countries increased to $18.2 billion in 2021-2022 against the US dollar. 10.8 billion in 2020-21.[3]

India and Bangladesh share 54 rivers. The Ganga Waters Treaty was signed in 1996 to share the water of the Ganga River during the harvest season (January 1 to May 31). Transport and trade through inland waterways are governed by a long-standing and proven protocol between Bangladesh and India. Energy sector cooperation between India and Bangladesh has also made significant progress recently. The India-Bangladesh Friendship Pipeline Project, signed in 2018, connects Siliguri, West Bengal, India and Parvatipur, Dinajpur District, Bangladesh. India and Bangladesh have also signed a Framework of Understanding (FOU) for cooperation in hydrocarbons.

The two countries are at a positive crossroads in their diplomatic relations after reaching a mutual understanding on maritime borders, land border arrangements, embargoed areas, short sea shipping and inland waterways. In this context, the celebration of India's Republic Day on January 26, 2021, has become a landmark event in the 50 years of diplomatic relations between India and Bangladesh. For the first time, a contingent of the Bangladesh Army consisting of 122 personnel from the three forces of the Army participated in the Republic Day Parade of

1. Ministry of External Affairs, India-Bangladesh Relations, Online Available at: https://mea.gov.in/Portal/ForeignRelation/Bangladesh_September_2017_en.pdf, Last accessed on October 03, 2022.
2. Ministry of External Affairs, India-Bangladesh Relations, Online Available at: https://mea.gov.in/Portal/ForeignRelation/Bangladesh_September_2017_en.pdf, Last accessed on October 03, 2022.
3. The Economic Times, "India Bangladesh Relations: Please do come and invest in Bangladesh: online Available at: https://auto.economictimes.indiatimes.com/news/industry/please-do-come-and-invest-in-bangladesh-tipu-munshi/94043262, Last accessed on October 03, 2022.

India. The event has preceded by a virtual meeting on December 17, 2020, and the two countries agreed to celebrate the golden anniversary of their diplomatic relations.[1]

India had always stood by Bangladesh when it needed help and economic support to deal with natural calamities and floods. Citizens of India has extended a credit line of $800 million to Bangladesh for various projects, including rail infrastructure, microprocessor-based locomotives and wagons, and purchasing buses and dredging projects. $150 million of the $200 million grant has already been delivered to Bangladesh in three instalments for use in high-priority projects for Bangladesh.[2]

Major issues between India and Bangladesh

In the following years, India and Bangladesh took great strides in promoting bilateral relations. But it was not a straight and upward path all along the way. Relations between the two countries has long been characterised by mistrust and suspicion. Still, the political will shown by the two countries top leaders has helped resolve some of the long-standing problems. Other important issues remain unresolved. In 2019, Prime Minister Narendra Modi said India-Bangladesh relations were in a "golden age" (Sonali Adhyay). The followings are the major issues between India and Bangladesh.

- Teesta River Water Dispute: The Teesta River flows from India through Bangladesh to the Bay of Bengal. Almost half a dozen districts in West Bengal depend on this river. It is also the primary source of irrigation for paddy fields that grow in the Rangpur district of Bangladesh. Bangladesh complains that it is not getting its share of water. Since water is a public entity in India, the bottleneck is in the lack of agreement between the state government of Bengal and the central Government.
- Illegal Migration: Illegal migration from Bangladesh to India, including refugees and economic migrants, continues unabated. Such a massive influx of migrants across the borders has created

1. Anasua Basu Ray Chaudhury, India-Bangladesh Relations @50 commemorating bilateral ties, Online Available at https://www.orfonline.org/series/india-bangladesh-relations-50-commemorating-bilateral-ties/
2. Ministry of External Affairs, India-Bangladesh Relations, Online Available at: https://mea.gov.in/Portal/ForeignRelation/Bangladesh_September_2017_en.pdf, Last accessed on October 03, 2022.

severe socio-economic and political problems for the people of the Indian states bordering Bangladesh, which will have severe implications for their resources and national security. Matters became more complicated when Rohingya refugees from Myanmar started entering India through Bangladesh.

- Drug and Human Trafficking: Cross-border drug and human trafficking occur frequently. Humans (especially children and women) has trafficked, and a wide variety of animals and birds have been hunted across borders.
- Terrorism: Borders are vulnerable to terrorist attacks. Many organisations like Jamaat Mujahideen Bangladesh (JMB) are trying to spread their tentacles across India. JMB is designated a terrorist group by Bangladesh, India, Malaysia and the UK. Recently, the National Bureau of Investigation filed a charge sheet against six JMB members in a special court in Bhopal.
- China's growing influence in Bangladesh: Bangladesh is now an active partner of the Belt and Road Initiative (BRI) (India is not part of the BRI). Bangladesh also imports Chinese military equipment, including submarines, in the defence sector, which is a significant concern for India's national security.

They are defining the extent of Teesta river water sharing and building consensus to reach a mutual agreement requires the Bengal government and the Central Government to work together with mutual understanding and show cooperative federalism. Connectivity in the region should be enhanced by strengthening cooperation in coastal connectivity, roads, railways and inland waterways. As the global energy crisis continues to intensify, India and Bangladesh must work together to use clean and green energy and make South Asia energy self-sufficient. Supporting Bangladesh with nuclear technology, artificial intelligence, modern agricultural technology, and flood data exchange will strengthen India-Bangladesh relations and help India counter China's influence. India and Bangladesh will take the initiative by encouraging other South Asian Countries for Regional Cooperation (SAARC) to establish specific procedures for determining the status of refugees and economic migrants and develop a SAARC Declaration on Refugees.

3.2.3 Indo-Bhutan Relations

The relationship between India and Bhutan is unique in many ways.

Compared to other bilateral relations with India's neighbours, relations with Bhutan are relatively smooth and friendly. India and Bhutan had shared links since 1910, when Bhutan became a protectorate of British India, allowing Britain to guide its foreign and defence policy.[1] When India declared its independence in 1947, Bhutan was among the first countries to recognise it. Since then, relations between the two countries have grown stronger. In addition to the common border of 699 km, India and Bhutan also have deep religious and cultural ties. Guru Padmasambhava, a Buddhist saint, played an influential role in spreading Buddhism and strengthening the traditional relationship between the people of the two countries.[2] Diplomatic relations between India and Bhutan were established in 1968 with the establishment of a particular office of India in Thimphu. The basic framework of bilateral relations between India and Bhutan is the Treaty of Friendship and Cooperation, signed between the two countries in 1949 and revised in February 2007.[3]

India has always been Bhutan's largest trading partner. Since 2014, trade between India and Bhutan has doubled from $484 million in 2014-15 to $183 million in 2020-21, accounting for more than 85 per cent of Bhutan's total trade, while India has the trade balance out.[4] Trade between the two countries has governed by the India-Bhutan Trade, Commerce and Transit Agreement, first signed in 1972 and revised for the fifth time in 2016.[5] India is the main source of investment in Bhutan, accounting for 47% of the country's total foreign direct investment. Bhutan is home to more than 40 Indian companies operating mainly in hydropower, finance, manufacturing, information technology and other service sectors.

India is Bhutan's leading development partner, and India has supported Bhutan's FYP since the inception of the first five-year program in 1961.

---

1. India's Place in the world,(2021) Policy Watch, Rajiv Gandhi Institute for Contemporary Studies, New Delhi Volume X, Issue 7.
2. Bhattacherjee Kallol, (FEBRUARY 03, 2019), 'Buddhism gives firmer ground for India-Bhutan relations", The Hindu, Online Retrieved From. https://www.thehindu.com/news/national/buddhism-gives-firmer-ground-for-india-bhutan-relations/article26167242.ece
3. MEA, Government of India, India-Bhutan Relations, Retrieved From: https://www.mea.gov.in/Portal/ForeignRelation/Brief_Bilateral_Brief_bhutan_Feb_2020.pdf
4. PIB, Government of India, Retrieved From; https://pib.gov.in/PressReleasePage.aspx?PRID=1769254
5. PIB, Government of India, "Trade Agreement between India and Bhutan", Retrieved From; https://pib.gov.in/newsite/PrintRelease.aspx?relid=154916

India has allocated Rs 4.5 billion for Bhutan's 12th fiscal year.[1] India plays a vital role in the development of hydropower projects. Besides supplying electricity to Bhutan, it also earns money by exporting surplus electricity to India. So far, the Government of India has constructed four large-scale hydropower projects (HEPs) in Bhutan with a total capacity of 2,136 MW, including 336 MW Chukha HEP, 60 MW Koricho HEP and 1,020 MW HEP in Bhutan. 720 MW Mandcho HEP. Two HEPs are currently under construction: 1200 MW Punatsangchhu-I HEP and 1020 MW Punatsangchhu-II HEP. In June 2020, a concession agreement was signed for the Kholongchu joint venture project in eastern Bhutan. The project is underway and has expected to be completed in 2026.[2]

Over the past decades, India has contributed significantly to the socioeconomic development of Bhutan by following the priorities and needs of the Bhutanese Government and the people of Bhutan. India's development assistance to Bhutan is mainly governed by an overarching mechanism of bilateral development cooperation consultations or annual planning consultations where both parties jointly determine the components and modalities of assistance.

The key areas of focus of India's assistance continue to be those that have a direct bearing on the lives of the common people. The scope of PTA projects ranges from agriculture to irrigation, ICT, media, health, tertiary education, school education, scholarships, labour and human resource development, roads, energy, urban development, judiciary, culture, constitutional offices and media.

Bhutan was the first country to receive the Made in India Covishield vaccines under the Ministry of External Affairs Vaccine Maitri Initiative. The first consignment of 150,000 vaccines was gifted on January 20, 2021. On March 22, 2021, the Government of India granted the second consignment of 400,000 doses of the 'Made in India' vaccines to the Royal Government of Bhutan in keeping with the uniquely close and friendly relations between both countries. A total of 550,000 doses of Covishield were given to Bhutan on a grant basis. In addition to 02 consignments,

---

1. MEA, Government of India, India-Bhutan Relations, Retrieved From: https://www.mea.gov.in/Portal/ForeignRelation/Brief_Bilateral_Brief_bhutan_Feb_2020.pdf
2. Huma Siddiqui (October 21, 2020), "Celebrating India-Bhutan ties: The Mangdechhu Hydroelectric Power Project receives prestigious award", The Financial Express, Online Retrieved From: https://www.financialexpress.com/infrastructure/celebrating-india-bhutan-ties-the-mangdechhu-hydroelectric-power-project-receives-prestigious-award/2110873/

the Government of India has delivered 11 medical consignments to Bhutan containing essential medicines, including Paracetamol, Cetrizine, Hydroxychloroquine and medical equipment, including PPE kits, N95 masks, RT-PCR test kits and 07 portable digital x-ray machines to Bhutan.[1]

The tradition of regular high-level meetings between the two countries maintains a unique traditional bilateral relationship characterised by trust and understanding. The current Prime Minister of India, Narendra Modi, chose Bhutan as his first foreign destination, stressing regional rather than global cooperation. During his visit, he met with His Majesty the King, the Fourth King and the Prime Minister of Bhutan for a comprehensive review of all aspects of bilateral relations. Prime Minister Modi and Prime Minister Lutai Tshering expressed their wish for an extraordinary state of bilateral relations based on mutual trust and respect and based on shared historical, cultural, economic, developmental and people-to-people ties. His Majesty, the King of Bhutan, has been awarded the Druk Gyalpo Medal (Ngadag Pel gi Khorlo), Bhutan's highest civilian award. The award recognises the Prime Minister's outstanding contribution to strengthening friendly relations between India and Bhutan. Prime Minister Modi is the first foreigner to receive this prestigious award from His Majesty the King of Bhutan.[2]

Bhutan is an important buffer state for India as it acts as a defense against China by defending the Chicken's Neck Corridor. Siliguri Corridor, or Chicken's Neck, is a narrow strip of land about 22 kilometers long. It is located in the Indian state of West Bengal, which connects the northeastern states of India with the rest of India. The countries of Nepal and Bangladesh are located along a corridor. The Doklam standoff reaffirmed Bhutan's strategic importance to India. Bhutan is also an essential part of India's neighborhood foreign policy. Bhutan also plays a crucial role in protecting India's Siliguri Corridor, a small strip of land that connects northeastern India with the rest of the country.[3]

India and Bhutan share a warm friendship, but China's ongoing claims over key border areas such as the Chumbi Valley and Doklam, as well

1. MEA, Government of India, India Bhutan Relations, Retrieved From: https://mea.gov.in/Portal/ForeignRelation/Bhutan_2021.pdf
2. PIB, Government of India, "PM honoured with Bhutan's highest civilian award" Retrieved From; https://pib.gov.in/PressReleaseIframePage.aspx?PRID=1782810
3. P. Stobdan, (2017), "In the Tri-Junction Entanglement, What Does Bhutan Want? "The Wire, Online Retrieved From https://thewire.in/diplomacy/bhutan-doklam-border-china

as China's efforts to establish strong diplomatic and economic ties with Bhutan, continue a constant source of concern for India.

While the economic and geographic size difference between the two neighbours makes Indo-Bhutan relations tilt in one direction, the truth is that this relationship is based on shared cultural values and authenticity. It is a mutually beneficial relationship based on the importance of friendship. Indian diplomacy has created deep political and economic ties with Bhutan. India and Bhutan have close and friendly relations supported by mutual trust and confidence. This relationship has helped Bhutan shape its development path based on Gross National Happiness (GNH). The indo-Bhutan relationship is perhaps the only bilateral relationship in South Asia with significant benefits for both sides. While Bhutan has appreciated India's economic assistance, India has shown sensitivity to Bhutan's development requirements.

3.2.4 India and Maldives Relations

India and Maldives share ethnic, linguistic, cultural, religious and trade ties steeped in antiquity and enjoy close, cordial and multidimensional relations. India was among the first to recognise the Maldives after its independence in 1965 and establish diplomatic relations with it. India launched its mission at the CDA level in 1972 and Resident High Commissioner in 1980. The Maldives opened a full-fledged High Commission in New Delhi in November 2004, one of its only four diplomatic missions worldwide.[1]

Both countries' bilateral relations have been strengthened with regular contact at the highest levels. Almost all Indian Prime Ministers have visited the Maldives since establishing diplomatic relations. Maldives was one of the first countries to support Sri Kamalesh Sharma's candidacy for the Secretary General of the UNO. Maldives was also a co-sponsor of the G4 draft resolution on UN reform. India has extended its support to Maldives' bid for a non-permanent seat on the UN Security Council for the 2019-2020 terms.[2]

India has supported the developmental process of the Maldives, such as (i) Indira Gandhi Memorial Hospital (IGMH) (ii) the Faculty of Engineering and Technology (FET). India and Maldives signed a trade agreement in 1981. In 2021, India will become Maldives' third largest

1. Ministry of External Affairs, GOI, "India and Maldives Relations", Online Retrieved From'; https://www.mea.gov.in/Portal/ForeignRelation/Maldives-January-2012.pdf
2. Ministry of External Affairs, GOI, "India and Maldives Relations", Online Retrieved From'; https://www.mea.gov.in/Portal/ForeignRelation/Maldives-January-2012.pdf

trading partner. Bilateral trade between India and Maldives will cross $300 million for the first time in 2021, taking the total to a staggering $323.29 million.[1] India's imports from the Maldives consist mainly of scrap metal, while India's exports to Maldives include agricultural and poultry products, sugar, fruits, vegetables, spices, rice, textiles, drugs and pharmaceuticals, various engineering and industrial products, Cement etc. India leads the tourism market with 132,151 tourists in 2022 (as of July 20, 2022), accounting for 14.7% of the market.

Since 1988, defense and security have been the main areas of cooperation between India and the Maldives. India has taken a very flexible and versatile approach to meet Maldives' defense training and equipment requirements. India offers the highest number of training opportunities to the Maldivian National Defense Force (MNDF).

India provided significant support to the Maldives during the aftermath of the 2004 Indian Ocean tsunami and the 2014 water crisis. A memorandum of understanding for cooperation in disaster management between the NDMAs of India and the NDMAs of Maldives was signed during President Soli's official visit to India from 1-4 August 2022.[2]

Maldives was also the first country to receive the covid vaccine. India's vaccine diplomacy is proof of the country's first neighbourhood policy, in which Maldives has a special and central position.

Greater Male Connectivity Project (GMCP)

Under the project, $400 million LoC and $100 million contribution from the Government of India, the GMCP project will connect Male to Villingili, Guruhifaru and Thilafushi islands through a series of bridges, causeways and roads. This project is important for the proposed Garifaru Port and will be a major catalyst for the Maldivian economy in the future through employment and economic activity. The project was awarded to AFCONS in August 2021. During President Solly's official visit to India on August 1-4, 2022, GMCP's first concrete loading marked the start of permanent work.[3]

1. High Commission of India,' India-Maldives Bilateral Relations', Online Retrieved From https://hci.gov.in/male/?pdf1185?000.
2. PIB, Government of India, Retrieved From https://pib.gov.in/PressReleaseIframePage.aspx?PRID=1857419
3. The Indian Express, (August, 26,2021), ' India, Maldives to sign pact on Greater Male Connectivity Project' Retrieved From https://indianexpress.com/article/india/india-maldives-greater-male-connectivity-project-7471603/

Challenges to the bilateral relations

India-Maldives relations are vital to Indo-Pacific maritime stability and security. As part of the Government's 'Neighbourhoods First' strategy, India remains a committed development partner for a secure, prosperous and peaceful Maldives. But Maldives also needs to continue with the 'India First' policy to maintain a strategic level of comfort in relations. Bilateral relations deteriorated during the presidency of Abdullah Yameen (2018-2013), especially with the rapid expansion of economic and strategic ties between Maldives and China.

India has made significant inroads in the Maldives, and the India Out campaign has gained momentum in the recent years. Former president Abdullah Yamin led the Chinese-backed campaign. Yamin, who was sentenced to five years in prison and fined five million dollars for embezzling one million dollars from the government budget, will be released from house arrest in 2021. The court also acquitted him of embezzlement charges due to insufficient evidence. These developments indicate Yameen's return to politics and can determine the fate of India-Maldives relations if Yameen wins the 2023 presidential election. To combat anti-India sentiment, Present President Soli signed an executive order in April this year declaring the India Out campaign a threat to national security and asking security agencies to crack down on dissidents who spearheaded the campaign.[1]

Another concern is the radicalisation of the Maldives. Over the past decade, more and more Maldivians have been recruited by terrorist groups such as the Islamic State (ISIS), Pakistan-based madrassas and jihadist groups. Islamic extremism is rising in this island nation, mainly due to political instability and social and economic uncertainty. Maldivian radicalisation has also been influenced by events in Pakistan, Afghanistan and West Asia. This increases the risk that Pakistan-based terrorist groups will use the remote islands of the Maldives as a launching pad for attacks against India and its interests.[2]

China's growing influence in the Maldives is a major concern for India due to the planned or ongoing implementation of a number of Chinese-led

1. The Indian Express, (March 30, 2022". 'Explained: What's behind the new anti-India campaign in the Maldives?' Retrieved From: https://indianexpress.com/article/explained/explained-whats-behind-the-new-anti-india-campaign-in-the-maldives-7838417/
2. Roshni Thomas,(2015), "Radicalism in the Maldives: Should India be worried?", The Institute of Peace and Conflict Studies (IPCS), Online Retrieved From: http://www.ipcs.org/comm_select.php?articleNo=4888.

investment projects. China's strategic presence in the region around India is expanding. A key "pearl" in China's "String of Pearls" strategy in South Asia has emerged as the Maldives. There are speculations that China is looking to establish strategic bases in the archipelago due to its strategic location in the Indian Ocean.[1]

However, Ibrahim Mohamed Solih's victory in the 2018 presidential elections turned Maldivian foreign policy orientation towards India. India proactively responded to this opportunity. Prime Minister Narendra Modi attended the oath-taking ceremony of Solih in November 2018. For his part, Solih chose India as the country of his first foreign visit as president in December 2018. Under Solih's presidency, Maldives also prioritised relations with India under the India First Policy. This policy has been complemented by India's Neighbourhood First Policy. India's sustained diplomatic, economic and strategic engagements with Maldives and Solih's favourable response to the same since his becoming president in 2018 have been crucial in India's counterbalance strategy against China in South Asia. [2]

Maldives is an important country in the Indian Ocean region for India. India's deep diplomatic, economic and strategic engagement with Maldives seeks to counter traditional and non-traditional security threats. It is very important for India to remain engaged and at the same time try to connect with the Maldivian people and make them more accepting. Such measures can help India maintain its geopolitical dominance in the Maldives.

India should play a key role in the Indo-Pacific security arena to ensure regional security in South Asia and its surrounding waters. The Indo-Pacific security environment has evolved in response to the growth of extra-regional powers (especially China) in India's maritime sphere of influence. Sustainable management and utilisation of maritime resources is essential for India's success in the blue economy, and the SAGAR vision (Security and Growth for All in the Region) [3]

1. Ashraf, Junaid. "String of Pearls and China's Emerging Strategic Culture." Strategic Studies, vol. 37, no. 4, 2017, pp. 166–81. JSTOR, https://www.jstor.org/stable/48537578. Accessed 7 Oct. 2022.
2. Niranjan Marjani, (2022), ' Continuity and challenges in the India-Maldives relations', Online Available at: https://www.wionews.com/continuity-and-challenges-in-the-india-maldives-relations-504965.
3. The Hindu, (April, 22, 2020), "Putting the SAGAR vision to the test" Online Available at: https://www.thehindu.com/opinion/op-ed/putting-the-sagar-vision-to-the-test/article31399219.ece

3.2.5 Indo-Nepal Relations

India-Nepal relations derive their strength from shared history, common cultural ethos, and long years of close and intense people-to-people contacts facilitated by open borders. Nepal is an important neighbor of India and, due to the geographical, historical, cultural, and economic ties that span centuries, occupies special importance in its foreign policy. Not only do the two countries share an open border and undisturbed movement of people, but they also have strong relations through marriages and family links. India- Nepal relations are, in essence, much more than the sum of treaties and agreements concluded between the two countries, however, The India-Nepal Treaty of Peace and Friendship of 1950 forms the bedrock of the special relations that exist between the two countries. Under the provisions of this Treaty, the Nepalese citizens have enjoyed unparalleled advantages and privileges in India, availing facilities and opportunities at par with the Indian citizens.[1] The Treaty has allowed Nepal to overcome the disadvantages of being landlocked.[2]

Nepal shares a border of over 1850 kms in the east, south and west with five Indian States -with 5 Indian states- Uttarakhand, Uttar Pradesh, West Bengal, Sikkim, and Bihar. Nepal is right in the middle of India's 'Himalayan frontiers', and along with Bhutan, it acts as northern 'borderland' flanks and acts as buffer states against any possible aggression from China.[3] Hence security-related issues are of prime concern to both the countries. The frequent high level visits by the leaders of the two countries at different points of time and the interactions constitute the hallmark of the ties between the two countries. Furthermore, such visits have helped promote goodwill, trust, understanding and cooperation between the two countries and, have injected fresh momentum to further consolidate age-old and multi-faceted bilateral relations of friendship and cooperation on a more mature and pragmatic footing. India has been a key development partner of Nepal. The latter received strong support and solidarity from

---

1. Mohan, Saumitra,(2017), *"Indian Policy and Development: A Manual of National Schemes and International Policies"*, McGraw Hill Education (India) Private Limited.
2. The Economic Times, (Aug 04, 2014), *'India, Nepal agree to review 1950 friendship treaty'*, Available Online at: https://economictimes.indiatimes.com/news/politics-and-nation/india-nepal-agree-to-review-1950-friendship-treaty/articleshow/39631792.cms?from=mdr, Last accessed on January, 31.2021.
3. Dalal, Saurabh.(2020), *"Relations between India and Nepal in covid-19 situation"*, Journal of Historical Archaeology & Anthropological Sciences, Volume 5 Issue 5, Available Online at : https://medcraveonline.com/JHAAS/JHAAS-05-00232.pdf, Last accessed on February, 03.2021.

the people and Government of India in advancing its home-grown peace process as well as in the process of writing the Constitution through the elected Constituent Assembly. Following the massive earthquakes in Nepal in April and May 2015, India promptly offered helping hands and also the first to supply Nepal with the COVID-19 vaccine. The Government of India has also been substantially supporting Nepal's reconstruction efforts.[1] India also Nepal's largest trade partner and the largest source of foreign investments.

However, Narendra Modi's election victory in May 2014 sent positive vibes across the SAARC region. His invitation to the Heads of Government of South Asian Association for Regional Cooperation (SAARC) for the swearing-in ceremony and his first official foreign visits to Bhutan and Nepal clearly emphasised his priority of India's neighbourhood.[2] Given his Neighbourhood First Policy and the importance that Nepal holds in India's strategic consideration, Prime Minister, Narendra Modi, visited Nepal four times during his tenure of six years, which reflects the priority that the Indian Government accords to its relations with Kathmandu.[3] In his first visit, Modi revised and adjusted the 1950 Indo-Nepal Treaty of Peace and Friendship as well as other bilateral agreements that were considered "unequal" by generations of Nepalese leaders. He also reactivated the joint commission, which was formed after a 23-year hiatus in 1987 at the level of foreign ministers. The aim of the commission is to strengthen, understand and promote cooperation between the two countries for mutual benefits in the economic, commercial and transportation sectors. Comprehensive use of water resources

Despite friendly relations in most cases, there are times when border disputes take a severe turn. The recent border dispute over the Kalapani region has affected bilateral relations between the two countries. Earlier, the riots in Madras, a region bordering India and Nepal, fueled anti-India sentiment among the ruling elite and led to deterioration in bilateral

1. Ministry of Foreign Affairs, Government of Nepal, *"Nepal-India Relations"*, Available Online at: https://mofa.gov.np/nepal-india-relations/, last accessed on February, 03.2021.
2. Pramod Jaiswal (2017) "Three Years Of The Modi Government India-Nepal Relations: Mixed Fortunes", Institute of Peace and Conflict Studies, Available Online at http://www.ipcs.org/comm_select.php?articleNo=5338, Last accessed on October, 03, 2022
3. Jha Haribansh, (2021) A reset of India–Nepal relations", Observer Research Foundation, Available Online At https://www.orfonline.org/expert speak/reset-india-nepal-relations/, Last accessed On October, 03, 2022

relations. India launched a nationwide "campaign of non-cooperation", and stopped importing fuel and other essential commodities from India to Nepal. Kathmandu's ruling elite claimed the "siege" was imposed with Indian support because India did not welcome Nepal's new non-inclusive constitution that sparked the Madhesi protests. These are the main issues in India-Nepal bilateral relations.

But India has tremendous influence in Nepal. It continues to be Nepal's largest trading partner and contributes greatly to the country's development. New Delhi has played a vital role in major political transitions in Nepal, including the overthrow of the autocratic Rana regime, Restoration of democracy in 1990, Abolition of the monarchy, or mainstream Maoists. This country should play a role in bringing stability and development to Nepal, which will ultimately serve India's main interest, i.e. security.

Meanwhile, China's growing role is weighing on the Nepal-India border dispute. India and Nepal should resolve their borders officially and amicably, and both countries should look deeply into history for a mutually beneficial and sustainable partnership to avoid past mistakes.

3.2.6 India–Pakistan Relations

India and Pakistan have had strained relations since India's independence and the partition of the two countries. India-Pakistan ties are one of the most complex associations that India shares with any of its neighbouring countries. Despite many contentious issues, India and Pakistan have significantly reduced the "trust deficit" over the past few years. India desires peaceful, friendly and cooperative relations with Pakistan, which requires an environment free of violence and terror. The two countries share linguistic, cultural, geographical and economic ties but share a complex relationship for political and historical reasons. Indo-Pak relations have been defined by the violent partition of British India in 1947, the Jammu and Kashmir conflict, and numerous military conflicts between the two nations. The history of Pakistan-India relations can be characterised as one of the lost opportunities. Mistrust, hostility and conflict have undermined efforts for peace and stability. Since independence, Pakistan and India have seen numerous wars, border skirmishes and military disputes. They also continue to have unresolved conflicts, lingering irritations, and a history of broken promises.[1]

1. See Details at India-Pak Relations – A brief history, The European Foundation for South Asian Studies (EFSAS), Online Available at: https://www.efsas.org/topics/indo-pak-relations.html, Last Accessed on, October, 05, 2022

Major issues in Indo-Pak Relations

The followings are the major issues in India-Pakistan Relations.

1. Cross-Border terrorism and ceasefire violations:

Cross-border terrorism has been an issue since independence. Terrorism emanating from territories under Pakistan's control remains a core concern in bilateral relations. India has consistently stressed the need for Pakistan to take credible, irreversible and verifiable action to end cross-border terrorism against India.[1] Pakistan is yet to bring the perpetrators of the 2008 Mumbai terror attack to justice in an ongoing trial, even after all the evidence is presented. India is adamant that it will not tolerate or create national security issues. Based on the attacks in India and the involvement of neighboring countries, the Indian Army, in response to the attacks on army camps in Uri, Jammu and Kashmir, conducted surgical strikes on various terrorist launch pads along the Line of Control. India again responded with an attack. Cross-border terror attack by Indian security forces in Pulwama with successful airstrike on JeM training camp in Pakistan's Balakot is one of the biggest confounding factors. Security is the biggest problem for India. After the 2008 Mumbai attacks, New Delhi broke off talks with Pakistan and refused to resume talks, saying Pakistan should do more against the rice plantations of Pakistan-based extremist groups. India has condemned the attacks by Pakistan-based militants and wants to show Islamabad that it is serious about deterring those behind the attack that killed 166 people. This is further complicated by India's claim that Pakistan's security services have somehow supported the militants.

Despite a ceasefire agreement in 2003 after the Kargil conflict, there have been regular ceasefire violations by Pakistan on the border since 2009, resulting in casualties among security forces and civilians on both sides. Widespread retaliation by the Modi government for Pakistan's ceasefire violations has increased the number of terrorist attacks from across the Southeast region. Subsequent incidents of the Patangkot and Oli attacks in 2016 prompted the Indian Prime Minister to declare that "talks and terrorism cannot go together" and called off efforts to hold bilateral talks between the two countries. This was followed by surgical strikes by the Indian Army across the LoC to target terrorist infrastructure in PoK. India's current position is that talks will not begin until Pakistan tackles cross-

1. Ministry of External Affairs, GOI, Online Available at: https://www.mea.gov.in/Portal/ForeignRelation/Bilateral_Brief_pakistan.pdf, Last Accessed on October, 05,2022.

border terrorism. On the other hand, Pakistan is ready to negotiate, but the issue of Kashmir is included.[1]

2. Kashmir Issue:

The Kashmir dispute is primarily a territorial dispute between India and Pakistan over the Kashmir region, with China playing a third role.[2] After the partition of India in 1947, conflict erupted as both India and Pakistan claimed the entire former kingdom of Jammu and Kashmir. This dispute over the region has turned into three wars between India and Pakistan and several other armed conflicts. India controls about 55% of the region's area, which includes Jammu, the Kashmir Valley, most of Ladakh and the Siachen Glacier. and 70% of its population. Pakistan owns about 30% of the country's territory, including Azad Kashmir and Gilgit-Baltistan. And China controls the remaining 15 percent of the land, including China's Aksai region, the largely uninhabited Trans-Karakorum route, and parts of the Demchuk sector.[3]

After the partition of India and a rebellion in the western districts of the state, Pakistani tribal militias invaded Kashmir, leading the Hindu ruler of Jammu and Kashmir to join India. The resulting Indo-Pakistani War ended with a UN-mediated ceasefire along a line that was eventually named the Line of Control. After further fighting in the wars of 1965 and 1971, the Simla Agreement formally established the Line of Control between the two nations› controlled territories.[4] In 1999, an armed conflict between India and Pakistan broke out again in Kargil with no effect on the *status quo*.

This is one of the most sensitive issues between India and Pakistan and the main reason for the strained relations between the two countries. Article 370 gave Jammu and Kashmir a special right to have its own constitution, independent flag and laws, but in August 2019[5], this article was revoked

1. **Omkar Dattatray/(October 2, 2018),** "Indo-Pak dialogue, Online Available at https://archive.statetimes.in/indo-pak-dialogue/, Last accessed on October,05, 2022.
2. Yahuda, Michael (2 June 2002). "China and the Kashmir crisis". BBC. Retrieved 22 March 2019.
3. Slater, Christopher L.; Hobbs, Joseph J. (2003). Essentials of World Regional Geography (4 ed.). Brooks/Cole Thomson Learning. p. 312. ISBN 9780534168100. LCCN 2002106314 – via Internet Archive. India now holds about 55% of the old state of Kashmir, Pakistan 30%, and China 15%.
4. "Simla Agreement". Bilateral/Multilateral Documents. Ministry of External Affairs, Government of India. Retrieved 27 September 2013.
5. BBC News, "Article 370: What happened with Kashmir and why it matters", Online Available at https://www.bbc.com/news/world-asia-india-49234708/ Last Accessed on October, 05, 2022.

and J&K now has the status of a union territory, a move that the Indian Government took seriously. With the opposition of Pakistan, which aspired to complete possession of Kashmir, a long-standing and critical problem awaited resolution. The unresolved conflict in Kashmir has proven to be a security threat in the South Asian region. India and Pakistan have fought many wars, but Kashmir has been the main motive behind these wars.

3. Water Issue

Water issue is an important issue between India and Pakistan Relations. The two countries disagree over the use of the water flowing down rivers that rise in Indian Kashmir and run into the Indus river basin in Pakistan. The use of the water is governed by the 1960 Indus Water Treaty under which India was granted the use of water from three eastern rivers, and Pakistan the use of three western rivers.[1] Pakistan says India is unfairly diverting water with the upstream construction of barrages and dams. India denies the charge.

4. Siachen Glacier

Siachen Glacier is located in the north of Ladakh in the Karakoram mountain range. This glacier is the fifth largest glacier in the Karakoram range and the second largest glacier in the world.[2] Most of the Siachen Glacier is contested between India and Pakistan. According to the Shimla Treaty of 1972, Siachen was declared sterile and useless. In this agreement, the border between India and Pakistan is not specified. When India received information that Pakistan was about to capture the Siachen Glacier, it launched Operation Megdout to reach the glacier first. After the success of Operation Meghdoot, Indian forces captured the area at higher altitudes, while Pakistani forces gained much lower altitudes. Therefore, India has a strategic advantage in the region.[3] After a ceasefire between the two countries in 2003, firing and shelling in the area stopped, but both countries maintained their forces in the area.

1. Press Information Bureau, Government of India, "Indus Waters Treaty 1960 : Present Status of Development In India', Online Available at: https://pib.gov.in/Pressreleaseshare.aspx?PRID=1565906#:~:text=Under%20the%20Indus%20Waters%20Treaty,to%20India%20for%20exclusive%20use., Last retrieved On October, 05, 2022.
2. The Times of India, (September 1, 2017),"Siachen—the world's highest battlefield", Online Available at; https://timesofIndia.indiatimes.com/travel/destinations/siachenthe-worlds-highest-battlefield/articleshow/45788658.cms,
3. The Indian Express, (April, 13, 2018), "Operation Meghdoot: 34 years ago, how India won Siachen " Retrieved from : https://indianexpress.com/article/explained/operation-meghdoot-34-years-ago-how-india-won-siachen-5135429/

Confidence Building Measures between India and Pakistan

Since partition, India and Pakistan have signed a number of agreements to build confidence and reduce tensions. Perhaps the most notable of these are the Nehru-Rikat Agreement (1951), Indus Waters Treaty (1960), Tashkent Agreement (1966), Kutch Implementation Agreement (1969), Shimla Agreement (1972) 1978, Salaldam Agreement (1978) and establishment of the Joint Commission. With the exception of the Joint Commission, the rest were either products of crisis or war and should have given a logical end to previous developments. CBM is an efficient tool to improve relations between countries, but trust between two countries is essential for its success. CBM is hard to create, but easy to confuse or abandon. Some continue to succeed, others abandoned.

Major Achievements

Some of the confidence-building measures taken to improve Indo-Pakistan relations are as follows:

Military CBMs

- The Agreement on the Prohibition of Nuclear Sites and Attacks on Facilities was signed in 1988 and ratified in 1990. The first exchange took Place on January 1, 1992.[1] Under the agreement, India and Pakistan will exchange lists of nuclear sites to prevent attacks on each other's nuclear facility, this practice continues to this day.
- In 1991, the Agreement on Prior Notification of Military Exercises, Exercises and Movement of Forces came into effect. The agreement played a key role in reducing tensions on both sides of the LoC.
- A communication link between the Pakistan Coast Guard and the Indian Coast Guard was established in 2005 to enable the exchange of basic information about fishermen caught straying in each other's waters.[2]
- A hotline between the two countries Director Generals of Military Operations (DGMO) has been in place since 1965 and was used

1. Ministry of External Affairs, GOI, Online Available at: https://mea.gov.in/press-releases.htm?dtl/34736/India+and+Pakistan+exchanged+list+of+Nuclear+Installations Last Accessed on October, 05, 2022.
2. Ministry of External Affairs, GOI, Online Available at: https://mea.gov.in/TreatyDetail.htm?1822, Last Accessed on October, 05,2022.

for unscheduled exchanges to discuss troop movements after the 9/11 attacks and de-escalation.[1]

Civil CBM

Most of these CBMs focused on improving human-to-human interactions. Here are some key items that have more or less stood the test:

- Delhi and Lahore bus services started in 1999. After the 2001 attack on the Indian Parliament, the service was suspended. Then in 2003, with the improvement of bilateral relations, bus services were resumed. The service was recently suspended in 2019 after the repeal of Articles 370 and 35A of the Constitution of India.[2]
- Samjauta Express launched after the signing of the Shimla Agreement, the Samjauta Express connects Lahore, Pakistan and Attari, India. After repeated interruptions, it was restarted after negotiations. It was suspended after Kashmir's special status was revoked in 2019.[3]
- The weekly bus service between Srinagar and Muzaffarabad started in 2014.
- India provided humanitarian aid to Pakistan after the 2005 earthquake. Pakistan has also provided relief in the past after the 2001 Gujarat earthquake.

Failures in the CBM process

Although there are hotlines connecting both military and political leaders in both countries, they have been scarcely used when required the most. The absence of communications has led to suspicions and accusations of misinformation. There is a disproportionate emphasis on military CBMs and inadequate recognition of several momentous non-military CBMs. Governments of both sides often use CBMs as political tools to win over specific constituencies, which can be very damaging in

---

1. Michael Krepon, (2017), "South Asia Confidence-Building Measures (CBM) Timeline", THE STIMSON CENTER, Retrieved from: https://www.stimson.org/2017/south-asia-confidence-building-measures-cbm-timeline/
2. The Hindu, (August, 12, 2019),"After Pakistan cancels Delhi-Lahore bus service, Delhi Transport Corporation follows suit" Online Available at: https://www.thehindu.com/news/national/delhi-lahore-bus-service-suspended/article29008742.ece
3. The Indian Express, (April, 11, 2019), " India cancels Samjhauta Express service after Pakistan suspends operations" Online Available at: https://indianexpress.com/article/india/india-pakistan-cancels-operation-of-samjhauta-express-5896475/

the long run. Public conciliatory statements, which are meant to be CBMs, can have the opposite effect if they are insincere.

Both sides now use propaganda through the media to justify each other's positions on conflicting issues. This has created misunderstanding, hatred and stereotypes among the people of both countries. This method is also used for the political interests of both countries without considering the welfare and peace needs of their people. However, facilitating travel between the two countries, facilitating the Visa regime, creating security for tourists, organising student and professor exchanges and inviting experts, intellectuals and artists to events to strengthen bilateral relations of both countries.

It is the ability of a country to shape the preferences of other countries through its political values, culture, and attractiveness and attractiveness of foreign policies. Actions that can be taken to promote soft diplomacy, soft diplomacy has improved the people-to-people relations between the two countries to some extent and reduced the tension between the two sides.

India adheres to the principle of "neighbourhood first" and wants normal neighborly relations with Pakistan. India's consistent position is that any dispute between India and Pakistan should be resolved peacefully in an atmosphere free from terrorism and violence. Pakistan is responsible for creating such an enabling environment. It is clear that India will not compromise on matters of national security and will take firm and decisive steps to counter any attempt to undermine India's security and territorial integrity.

The failure of SAARC was mostly due to differences and tensions between India and Pakistan. Improved relations between India and Pakistan will ensure that any future threats the Indian subcontinent may face can be addressed. Cooperation and coexistence based on trust can ensure the establishment of a peaceful and prosperous South Asia.

3.2.7 India-Sri Lanka Relations

The relationship between India and Sri Lanka is centuries old. Both countries have a legacy of intellectual, cultural, religious and linguistic interaction. The relationship has been marked by close contacts at all levels in recent years. Trade and investment have grown, and there is cooperation in infrastructure development, education, culture and defense. India was among the first countries to recognise an independent Sri Lanka in 1948 and establish diplomatic relations with the island nation.[1]

Almost 30 years of armed conflict between the Sri Lankan Army and the LTTE ended in May 2009. During the conflict, India supported the Sri Lankan government's right to act against terrorist forces. India's steadfast position has been in favor of a negotiated political solution that is acceptable to all communities within the framework of an integrated Sri Lanka and consistent with democracy, pluralism and respect for human rights. India has helped Sri Lanka a lot during the recent economic crisis. Sri Lanka is one of India's largest trading partners among SAARC countries. India is Sri Lanka's largest trading partner in the world. India's exports to Sri Lanka reached $5.3 billion from 2015 to 2017, while imports from Sri Lanka reached $743 million. Since the signing of the India-Sri Lanka Free Trade Agreement, which took effect in March 2000,[2] trade between the two countries has expanded particularly rapidly. Sri Lanka and New Delhi have a long history of security cooperation. In recent years, the two countries have steadily strengthened their military-to-military relations. India and Sri Lanka conduct joint military exercises ("Mitra Shakti") and naval exercises (LINEX). India also provides defense training to the Sri Lankan Army. In April 2019, India and Sri Lanka also signed an agreement to combat drug and human trafficking.

Issues and concerns

Traditionally, bilateral relations between India and Sri Lanka have focused on a few specific issues and concerns – security concerns (now including security cooperation), ethnic issues, fisheries disputes, investment, environment, etc. However, India-Sri Lanka relations are moving away from traditional concerns and partnerships due to dynamic changes in the strategic environment in South Asia and the IOR. There is nothing to suggest that China's business investments over the past few years have led to a military/security nexus that New Delhi should worry about.[3]

1. Singhal Soumya ,(2021), "Long Lost Lanka: Reorienting India-Sri Lanka Relations Amidst Chinese Expansionism", Social and Political Research Foundation..
2. High Commission of India, "India-Sri Lanka Economic And Trade Engagement", Online Available at https://hcicolombo.gov.in/Economic_Trade_Engagement, Last accessed on October, 03 2022.
3. Moorthy N. Sathiya(2022), "Sri Lanka: Growing bilateral relations with India under President Wickremesinghe", Observer Research Foundation, Online Available at : https://www.orfonline.org/expert-speak/sri-lanka-growing-bilateral-relations-with-india/, Last accessed on October, 03. 2022.

China was at risk of investing heavily in unviable economic projects in Sri Lanka. Sri Lanka currently owes China $8 billion and is struggling to repay it. After the $1.6 billion Hambantota port was identified as a liability, Sri Lanka agreed to pay $1.12 billion for an 85 percent stake in Hambantota Port over 99 years,[1] state-owned China Merchants Port Holdings I signed a deal with the company (CMPort).). India is anxiously watching China take control of the Hambantota port to justify China's strategic presence in India's sphere of influence in the Indian Ocean.

China now has not only military superiority, but also commercial superiority in South Asia. After the China-Sri Lanka Free Trade Agreement (FTA) is finalised, Chinese companies can take advantage of India's free trade agreement with Sri Lanka to enter the Indian market. In this complex environment, two major issues emerge: the management of China's strategic power play in Sri Lanka and the management of the jihadist terrorist threat in Sri Lanka. China's established maritime assets in the IOR, including Hambantota, now stretch from Djibouti in the west to the South China Sea in the east. This is a challenge not only to India's strategic mix, but also to the US, Japan and their allies in the Pacific. They have united to create a collective power to meet the challenges posed by an increasingly assertive China. Now, after the ascension of the new Government, Beijing may have to bend backwards to prove to Sri Lanka and Sri Lankans that it did not desert a 'friend in need in its real hour of economic crisis. Even otherwise, given the current economic situation, the revival of the much-hyped, China-funded Colombo Port City project any time soon looks suspect at best.

However, India and Sri Lanka should look for ways to facilitate people-to-people contact. The largest tourists of this island nation come from India, but the extent of religious tourism has not yet been explored. Through Prime Minister Modi's $15 million grant to promote Buddhist ties with Sri Lanka announced last year, the two countries will be able to create a corridor of Buddhist knowledge and tourism. Finally, we need to capitalise on the glory and prevalence of cricket in both countries. The expansion of the Indian Premier League (IPL) to Sri Lanka in partnership

---

1. The Hindustan Times, (June, 26, 2022)," Was cash strapped Sri Lanka duped by China in Hambantota Port?" Online Available at : https://www.hindustantimes.com/world-news/was-cash-strapped-sri-lanka-duped-by-china-in-hambantota-port-101656205405799.html, Last accessed on October, 03,2022.

with the Sri Lankan Premier League (LPL) will promote people-to-people contact and boost tourism.[1]

Cooperation in these areas does not ease concerns about issues where the two neighbors may disagree: the rights of the Tamil minority and the importance of China to Sri Lanka's economy. However, history, cultural proximity and geographical limitations have made India and Sri Lanka as natural and permanent partners to overcome these problems and create new opportunities to jointly advance their economic and development aspirations. Two countries are democratic institutions, so there is room to expand and deepen our relations. Both countries should seek a lasting solution to the problem of fishermen through bilateral interaction. In order to improve the economic cooperation between the two countries, the Comprehensive Economic Partnership Agreement (CEPA) should be signed. Mutual recognition of each other's concerns and interests can improve the relations between the two countries.

---

1. Sappani Vijay,(2021), 'Charting a New Trajectory in India-Sri Lanka Relations"**, Observer Research Foundation, Online Available at** https://www.orfonline.org/expert-speak/charting-a-new-trajectory-in-india-sri-lanka-relations/, **Last accessed on October, 03.2022.**

Chapter - 4

India's Role and Contributions to SAARC

4.1 Introduction

The establishment of SAARC in 1985 was a turning point in the institutionalisation of regional cooperation in South Asia. The region has betrayed the institutionalisation of regional cooperation in South Asia. This area betrayed an apparent paradox. Although it is rich in human and natural resources, it also suffers from poverty. SAARC aims to accelerate the socio-economic development of its member countries through "collective self-reliance".[1] Thus, the creation of SAARC raised hopes among South Asians for a better situation characterised by prosperity and freedom from poverty.

Since the inception of SAARC, India has played a leading role in advancing its goals. India's contribution to SAARC is immense, from fundraising to sharing technical know-how. India is home to several SAARC institutions. India is the only country that shares a border with all SAARC members, except present-day Afghanistan. India scores very well in all areas compared to other regional association members. But when Prime Minister Modi invited SAARC heads of state to his inauguration ceremony, SAARC suddenly became more important. The Modi government is currently focused on strengthening ties with India's neighbours.

---

1. Jain, Romi. "India and SAARC: An Analysis." *Indian Journal of Asian Affairs*, vol. 18, no. 2, 2005, pp. 55–74. *JSTOR*, http://www.jstor.org/stable/41950459. Accessed October 14 2022.

4.2 India's Role in SAARC

India is the largest SAARC economy and has the most influence in economic matters. India also dominates SAARC in terms of geography, land size, population and political influence. India is an active member of SAARC and aims to promote better mutual understanding by supporting people-to-people initiatives. India is a significant potential investment in trade and commerce as it is the only SAARC member that shares land or sea borders with all six member countries except Afghanistan.[1] India is one of the founding member countries of SAARC and hosts two regional centres in this organisation, SAARC Documentation Center and SAARC Disaster Management Center. In addition, India is a permanent member of the SAARC Board, and Indian representatives have twice served as Executive Directors of the organisation. India has been a permanent member of SAARC since its inception, and Indian representatives were heavily involved in drafting the Charter, which was eventually signed by all countries. India also frequently hosts SAARC committee members when they meet for organisational summits. For example, the 1986 summit, in which the duties of the SAARC secretariat were revised and expanded, was held in Bangalore, India. In 2007, the 14th SAARC Summit was held in Delhi, India. This summit was notable because it marked the first time a new country was invited to become a member of SAARC when representatives from Afghanistan signed the Charter.[2]. Today, there is a significant increase in trade, connectivity and economic cooperation between India with other SAARC countries. In addition, India's annual contribution to the SAARC Development Fund (SDF) has increased over the previous year. India has hosted three of the 18 SAARC summits held so far. 2nd (Bangalore, November 1986), 8th (New Delhi, May 1995), 14th (New Delhi, April 2007). India is firmly committed to sharing the fruits of technological progress with its like-minded neighbours. In this context, the initiative to expand India's National Knowledge Network (NKN) to South Asian countries has also been extended to Sri Lanka, Bangladesh and Bhutan. India's Prime Minister launched an extension to Bhutan in August 2019. Expansion to other SAARC member countries is

1. Jangir, Mamta, (2017), *"India and South Asian association for regional Cooperation"* International Journal of Applied Research, Vol. 3, Issue. 3, pp. 912-914, Online Available at: http://www.allresearchjournal.com/archives/2017/vol3issue3/Part N/3-4-36-354.pdf
2. Kumar Revanth. G & Pokharel, (August 2016), *"Appraisal of India's bilateral trade relationship With SAARC countries"* Intercontinental Journal of Finance Research Review, Volume 4, Issue 8.

underway. India launched its South Asia Satellite (SAS) in May 2017 from Sriharikota. SAS demonstration terminals have been installed in Bhutan, Maldives, Afghanistan, Nepal, Bangladesh and Sri Lanka. For India, the region's largest economy, building an environment of trust among SAARC partners is both a necessity and an opportunity. This will encourage a greater commitment to regional integration among all countries.[1]

4.2.1 India's Role in SAARC under P.M Narendra Modi

The so-called Gujral Doctrine, wherein Former Prime Minister I.K. Gujral outlined five principles for managing India's relations with its neighbours, Gujral argued that as the dominant power in South Asia, India was sensitive to the concerns of its smaller neighbours and should pursue reconciliation and mediation to promote friendly relations with countries in the region.[2] Successive governments, especially those led by Prime Ministers Atal Bihari Vajpayee, Manmohan Singh and now Prime Minister Modi, have continued to engage with India's neighbours in this spirit. The current Prime Minister, Narendra Modi, has boldly raised new hopes for the future of SAARC. Narendra Modi and his government's aggressive foreign policy commitments ushered in a new era in India-SAARC relations. Prime Minister Narendra Modi has prioritised strengthening ties with India's neighbours. The gesture of inviting the South Asian Association for Regional Cooperation (SAARC) leader to his inauguration may be seen as symbolic. Still, it is the necessary push to bring SAARC to the forefront of India's foreign policy vocabulary. During the Nepalese Prime Minister's visit to India, Modi described SAARC as "an important tool to enhance the power of each member country and promote joint action for common prosperity in the region"[3]. Modi is widely seen as a reformist prime minister and is expected to open up the economy and liberalise trade. In addition, this agreement, which comes from a visit to neighbouring countries, shows a certain mentality of cooperation, especially in infrastructure and energy, intending to solve common problems. Therefore, it is logical for governments to explore similar opportunities to expand and deepen their

1. Sawhney, Aparna and Kumar, Rajiv, (2008), *"Rejuvenating SAARC: The Strategic Payoffs for India"*, Global Economy Journal, Volume 8, Issue 2.
2. Nadkarni, Vidya. (2014), *"India and SAARC"*, Prepared for presentation at the FLASCO ISA meeting, Buenos Aires, Argentina, July 24-26, Online Available at: http://web.isanet.org/Web/Conferences/FLACSOISA%20BuenosAires%202014/Archive/1226fcdb-083a-4d19-97bb-6f95cdd84685.pdf
3. Sidhu, W.P.S & Sandhu Rohan. (2014) *"Reinvigorating SAARC India's Opportunities and Challenges"*, Brookings India.

engagement with SAARC. The Prime Minister said at the 18th SAARC Summit: Prime Minister Narendra Modi at the 18th SAARC Summit in Nepal.

India has been an active member from the very beginning of SAARC and has played a crucial role in improving healthy and cordial relations among the SAARC countries. The Kashmir dispute between India and Pakistan is the prime cause of the ineffectiveness of SAARC in integrating South Asian countries. The SAARC members could benefit if there were a healthy relationship between India and Pakistan. The success of SAARC will hinge on an enduring peace between the two major powers- India and Pakistan- in the region as well as the determination of the leaders to strengthen the SAARC in promoting shared regional interests. However, India will continue to emphasise enhancing regional trade and cooperation as well as people-to-people contact. It needs to be emphasised that it is time for India to take steps to provide direction to the regional organisation to play a meaningful role by taking an active interest in its promotion. India has a stake in taking its leadership forward in the South Asian region for mutually rewarding regional cooperation. Regionalism through SAARC would be an important vehicle to carry forward India's dream for the region.

4.3 India's Contributions to SAARC

SAARC was established to improve many people's lives in South Asia by promoting economic cooperation among member countries. India is a regional superpower due to its size, population, military might, natural resources, technological and scientific advancements. India ranks first in terms of area, population and GNP. India has played a significant role in promoting the activities of SAARC since the beginning. The Bangalore summit approved the decision to establish a secretariat. India's contribution to SAARC Secretariat and expenditure on SAARC activities shows that in 1988, India contributed US$ 118,873 to SAARC activities and committed the largest tonnage to SAARC food reserves. This country plays a leading role in the field of cooperation. Right from the origin and evolutionary growth of SAARC, India has been playing a prominent role in it.

Here to assess India's Cooperation and Contributions to the SAARC are:

4.3.1 India and Economic Co-Operation in SAARC

One of the main goals of establishing the SAARC Forum was to accelerate the member countries' economic and social development.

Subsequently, trade promotion was also actively pursued as an area of economic cooperation. The potential of trade expansion in SAARC has been investigated using regional and macroeconomic trade linkage models. Overall, we find considerable room for further expansion of regional trade due to differences between countries in production and consumption patterns, investment behaviour and tax and non-tax structures. Currently, trade within SAARC is significantly lower than in regional bodies such as the European Union (E.U.) and the Association of Southeast Asian Nations (ASEAN).[1]

4.3.1.1 India's Role in Facilitating Trade under SAFTA

Trade and investment flow play an important role in the economic integration of the rest of the world, and South Asia can do the same. Compared to other economic regions such as Europe, North America and Southeast Asia, South Asia has not achieved the necessary economic growth and prosperity. Still, it has high economic power regarding market potential (a third of the human population lives in this region), abundant natural resources, and talented manpower. The world's poorest South Asian countries cannot sustain SAARC as a meaningless alliance. What is needed now is to put aside the bilateral conflicts and turn SAARC into a strong economic bloc. In this context, progress towards SAFTA is crucial. However, to benefit from increased regional trade, all SAARC member countries must prepare for the new challenges of free trade zones. India's importance in ensuring the success of SAFTA stems from its geographic location and economic size at the heart of the region.[2]

India is the largest economy in South Asia and accounts for more than 80% of South Asia's GDP. More than 90% of the regional trade of Bangladesh, Nepal and Sri Lanka and most of the world trade is with India. Trade between the rest of South Asia is much lower than India's trade with its South Asian partners. India's position at the geographical centre of the region means that it facilitates and transits all regional trade. We also steer the issue. Thus, the pace and direction of economic integration in South Asia will largely depend on India's relations with other economies in the region.[3]

1. Rajeev Jain and J. B. Singh (2009), 'Trade Pattern in SAARC Countries: Emerging Trends and Issues', Reserve Bank of India Occasional Papers, Vol. 30, No. 3.
2. Rahman et al. (2012),' Regional integration and economic development in South Asia, A JOINT PUBLICATION OF THE ASIAN DEVELOPMENT BANK AND EDWARD ELGAR PUBLISHING.
3. Rajiv Kumar and Manjeet Singh, (2009), 'India's Role in South Asia Trade and Investment Integration', ADB Working Paper Series on Regional Economic Integration XXX.

India has strengthened bilateral relations with its neighbours by signing free trade agreements with Nepal, Bhutan and Sri Lanka and a preferential trade agreement with Afghanistan. In 2006, India, along with Bangladesh, Bhutan, Maldives, Nepal, Pakistan and Sri Lanka, signed the South Asian Free Trade Agreement (SAFTA) under the auspices of the South Asian Association for Regional Cooperation (SAARC). One of the main elements of the agreement was the reduction of tariffs by all member countries under the Tariff Liberalization Program (TLP). However, items on the confidential list of member states are excluded. Member States also agreed to eliminate non-tariff and non-tariff barriers and adopt trade facilitation measures to remove barriers to the movement of goods across borders.

In recent years, India has taken several measures, both bilaterally and under the ambit of SAFTA, to facilitate trade in the region. Several initiatives have been implemented to liberalise the tariff regimes facing imports from South Asia and to address non-tariff barriers and transport impediments. However, Intra-SAARC trade continues to be very low (at about 5 per cent of the region's total trade), and India's imports from the rest of South Asia are less than 1% of its total imports. This is largely due to the high transaction costs incurred while moving goods across the borders in the region. The strained relations between India and Pakistan, the two largest economies in the region, have also prevented fruitful implementation of the major chunk of trade-facilitating measures in the region.[1].

4.3.1.2. Liberalisation of Tariffs under SAFTA and India's Bilateral FTAs

In accordance with the provisions of SAFTA, India has offered tariff concessions separately to NLDCs and LDCs. India also maintained separate rules of origin and sensitive lists for these two groups of countries. However, the concessions offered by the NLDC only apply to Pakistan as India has an FTA with Sri Lanka, and any LDC concessions only apply to Bangladesh as it is the only LDC member of SAFTA with which India does not have an FTA free trade. (Maldives is too small and accounts for only 0.1 per cent of the GDP of SAARC member countries).

Hence, from India's point of view, all the tariff liberalisation efforts with its SAARC members are bilateral. Negotiations with Sri Lanka, Nepal and

1. Nisha Taneja et al. (2013), 'India's Role in Facilitating Trade under SAFTA', INDIAN COUNCIL FOR RESEARCH ON INTERNATIONAL ECONOMIC RELATIONS.

Afghanistan are ongoing under the respective bilateral trade arrangements. Tariff negotiations are underway with Pakistan under SAFTA for NLDCs – and with Bangladesh under SAFTA for LDCs.[1]

4.3.1.3 Recent India's Economic Activities

- India has so far contributed over US$ 530. - Million to SAARC institutions for socio-economic development. India's trade with South Asia accounts for around 5.5% of its global trade. India has been advocating expedited negotiations/implementation of agreements, promoting investments, trade, and exchanges in the region. India's emphasis is on three central themes of SAARC- trade, connectivity and people-to-people contact.[2]
- The fledgling SAARC Development Fund (SDF) finances sub-regional projects envisaged under its social, economic and infrastructure windows. India is the only country to have paid its assessed contribution (for the entire 5-year period) of US$ 89.9 million and a voluntary contribution of US$ 100 million.[3]
- A currency swap arrangement for the region, with a base fund of US$ 2 billion from India, provides short-term foreign exchange liquidity requirements of Member States.
- India has set up a Special Purpose Facility(SPF) to finance infrastructure projects in the region that would enhance our connectivity and trade.
- India has given five South Asian partners duty-free access to 99.7% of their goods and is "prepared to do more with others".[4]
- Over the past decade, India has provided economic assistance of nearly US$ 8 billion to its South Asian neighbours.

So far, the scope of economic cooperation between South Asian states is limited to a few relatively insignificant and non-controversial areas. Vital

1. Ibid
2. Anil Trigunayat, (2017) India and the SAARC: Implications for the neighbourhood, MEA, Government of India. Online Retrieved From https://www.mea.gov.in/distinguished-lectures detail.htm?655.
3. MEA, Government of India, Online Retrieved From, https://www.mea.gov.in/Images/amb1/SAARC_Development_Fund2020.pdf
4. The Indian Express, (November 2, 2014),' Narendra Modi proposes special facility for funding SAARC infra projects', online Retrieved From; https://indianexpress.com/article/india/india-others/narendra-modi-proposes-special-facility-for-funding-saarc-infra-projects/.

areas such as foreign trade have not been given the attention they deserve. A lot can be achieved by working together in this area, and India can provide a ready market for a range of products and, in return, provide technical expertise to member states at a much cheaper cost. Overall, South Asia appears to have neglected India as an important customer and subsequently lost the benefits it could have gained from developing relations with a large country like India. It would be necessary to emphasise that if regional trade and economic cooperation are to be a reality, India must take the lead as an important industrial trading partner.

4.3.2 Education Sector

Writing about education in the South Asian region means writing about a quarter of the world's population. This region is rich in history and home to one of the oldest civilisations in the world. The ancient scriptures associated with this region placed education and knowledge on a high pedestal and considered it the most important treasure a person could have. Even at the beginning of the 21st century, many people in this region highly value education. Some of these countries were once very rich, industrial and materially prosperous. The importance of education is increasingly recognised in all countries of the region. The important role of education in social, economic and political development is widely recognised as a development tool and criterion. The result was an explosion of education in most developing countries in the second half of the 20th century. Realising the important role of education and the need to prioritise it in development efforts, most South Asian countries have begun to pay serious attention to it.

4.3.2.1 South Asian University

India hosts the prestigious South Asian University. It is committed to providing 100% of its capital costs, including 100 acres of land for its permanent campus in New Delhi.[1] The Prime Minister of India proposed establishing the South Asian University (SAU) at the 13th SAARC summit in Dhaka in 2005. The idea was for member countries to pool their resources for the creation of a Centre of Excellence in the form of a University that would provide world-class facilities and professional faculty to students and researchers drawn from every country of the SAARC region.

1. The Hindu, (January 19, 2022), 'South Asian University remains without president online Retrieved From: https://www.thehindu.com/education/colleges/south-asian-university-remains-without-president/article38293020.ece

It was established by the intergovernmental agreement of the 14th SAARC Summit (April 2008) to provide world-class educational facilities and professional faculty to students and researchers of SAARC countries. The University offer Master's and M.Phil/PhD programs in 8 disciplines. The University operates in a temporary facility in Akbar Bhawan, New Delhi. India has committed to cover all the capital costs for the permanent construction of the permanent campus on over 100 acres of land in Maidan Garhi, Delhi. This University plans to move to a permanent campus in the near future. SAU's operational budget is based on contributions from all SAARC member countries, with India being the largest contributor. India is offering SAARC LDC students 100 paid scholarships in South Asian universities.

India also offers postgraduate and PhD scholarships at the Indian Forest Institute, Dehradun. In addition, India offers two scholarships to each member country every year through ICCR under the SAARC Chair, Fellowships and Scholarship Scheme.

4.3.2.2 The National Knowledge Network (NKN)

The government is in the process of extending India's National Knowledge Network to SAARC countries in order to enhance cooperation in the field of education. The National Knowledge Network (NKN) is a state-of-the-art multi-gigabit pan-India network for providing a unified high-speed network backbone for all knowledge-related institutions in the country.

India's tele-education project for SAARC countries benefits the target student community.[1]

4.3.3 Science and Technology Cooperation

India is the advanced state of the South Asia Region in almost all spheres of life. Therefore it has been the moral responsibility of India to transfer the technical know-how to help build infrastructure to provide training facilities to the new entrepreneurs, provide technical information and knowledge, and arrange seminars, workshops and conferences from time to time. India organised various training courses for transferring technology to benefit SAARC member states.

1. The Hindu, June 9 03, 2015),' National Knowledge Network to be extended to SAARC countries' Online Retrieved From: https://www.thehindu.com/news/national/national-knowledge-network-to-be-extended-to-saarc-countries-sushma-swaraj/article7278560.ece.

4.3.3.1 Survey of Natural Resources and Remote Sensing

India is the first among the SAARC member states to launch a geological survey, mineral survey, agricultural and forestry survey, animal and husbandry survey, and remote sensing satellite for mineral as well as agricultural resources survey. India is the only country that has launched a Satellite Earth Observatory (SEO) System. Indian Space Research Organisation has launched satellites into space from domestically developed rockets. The Indian Space Research Organization (ISRO) has to bear the largest brunt. There is no alternative for the SAARC countries except to work closely with India's space programme because the data obtained by ISRO Satellite for Earth observation can be made available to the countries of the region." Thus India is the only .channel among the SAARC member states for high technology transfer to other members of the SAARC, and it is true also regarding natural resources, tapping of natural resources and conversion of it into produce codes and remote sensing.

4.3.3.2 Mining and Ore Beneficiation

The Indian subcontinent is rich in minerals, and all SAARC countries have a number of minerals. Himalaya is a common mountain which covers Bhutan, Nepal, the North Eastern and North Parts of India, and its Hindukush and Karakoram ranges are spread over Pakistan.

India is a leading country in land and sea minerals exploration. It provides technical know-how along with the sciences of experts, infrastructure, tools and machines to the seven member states of the SAARC Mining, a basic process for acquiring raw material in the form of mineral ore. Mineral ore is to be processed to acquire minerals in purified form. Then these ores are treated to convert into raw materials used in industrialisation to produce quality goods in a short period.

Indian technology is given to other SAARC member states for exploring and converting mineral ores into industrial raw materials. Under the SAARC scheme, India will help SAARC members establish small and medium industries. India uses raw materials in the form of mineral ore in its heavy industry. To some extent, Pakistan, Sri Lanka and Bangladesh are capable of mining. Iron Ore, Bauxite, Manganese, uranium 235 and 239 etc., are available in abundance.[1]

1. Shahid Kardar, (2011),' South Asia—Intraregional Cooperation: The Way Forward, Asian Development Bank.

4.3.3.3 Micro Electronics

Microelectronics is a product of the second industrial revolution. Only India, among the eight member states of SAARC, used the second industrial revolution to acquire professionalism in Micro - Electronics. Besides, India and Pakistan acquired moderate technology professionally in microelectronics. Remaining all other member states are lagging in electronics Maldives, Bhutan, Nepal, Bangladesh and Sri Lanka never classified electronics as a priority area. In contrast, India is at par with the most developed countries in microelectronics technology and industry.

India shares its enrichment with other SAARC countries. India presented a proposal come-draft that deals with ventures in several areas of electronics, such as computer technology, satellite technology, microchip technology, telecommunication technology etc., in which microelectronics is being used as a base. SAARC has partially accepted India's proposal and limited them to entertainment electronics. Today SAARC programmes are telecasted through Indian satellites in the South Asian Region.

India has established Regional Centre for Science and Technology for SAARC. Delhi is providing training for personnel of other SAARC states in computer handling and maintenance. This centre is also providing techno-economic exercises and the feasibility of computers for their economic development. Through computers, member states can gather data and information they need for their development. Micro Electronics Technology is the 21" Century technology tor SAARC member states, and the exception is only India.

4 .3.3.4 Genetic Engineering

South Asia Region is a backward region concerning modernisation and development, except for India. Genetic Engineering has progressed up to cloning in the most developed state, and SAARC members are at the primary level in this regard. The development programme in this region is related to improving the quality of crops and livestock. Therefore Genetic Engineering of the SAARC is restricted to agriculture, land and animal husbandry.

Through its research in agriculture and animal husbandry, India has reached such a state from which it can dictate the improvement and development of crops along with an increase in their yield. Wheat, rice, potatoes, tomatoes etc., are the crops given priority in Genetic Engineering.

In cross-breeding of domestic animals, artificial insemination technology is used and with the services rendered by Indian artificial insemination Centres and Hospitals for treating animals started functioning in the five member states of the SAARC, i.e. Nepal, Bhutan, Maldives, Bangladesh and Sri Lanka.

Indian agriculture universities, with the additional financial help of the Central Government, State Government and UNESCO, have developed and created wide varieties of various crops, including hybrid crop seeds, and technical know-how related to their farming is also passed to the member state, thereby giving then the benefit of the membership of SAARC through its extended programme in Genetic Engineering under science and technology committee.[1]

4.3.4 Telecommunication Sector:

India, the most advanced state in the field of TLC, has taken the initiative to impart technical knowledge to the other seven member states of the SAARC. India organised a seminar on 'Latest trends in external Plant practices from 17th to 21st November 1986 and a seminar cum-workshop on 'Software maintenance in developing countries from 6th to 10th Oct.1987.India also organised a training course on 'General software development environment and facilities from October 26 to November 6 1987.

With the impetus provided by SAARC, India commissioned International Sub Scribes Dialing with Bangladesh, Sri Lanka, Nepal and Pakistan. India has also offered its network to SAARC member states wishing to give it for transit traffic. Furthermore, India has taken the initiative and complied with the activity of opening bureau fax services and augmentation of inter-country links in which all the eight member states of SAARC cooperate.

As a result of the cooperation in this area, ISD, Services are available in all member states. The native of one member state can make use of ISD telephone and automatic telex service; to have contact with the natives of other member states. Bureau fax service is already introduced in all member states of SAARC, and common collection charges and media-independent tariff has been introduced in the member states.

1. Ministry of Agriculture & Farmers Welfare, GOI, 'Promotion of Agricultural Research,' Online Retrieved From: https://www.pib.gov.in/PressReleasePage.aspx?PRID=1654495

4.3.5 Meteorology

The expertise attained by Indian Meteorology Departments/Institutes is utilised in the development plans of the SAARC region. Much progress is attained in this region due to India's contribution to establishing meteorological study centres in some of the Member states. The Indian knowledge is utilised for the benefit of all the Member states. India successfully shouldered the responsibilities bestowed upon it by SAARC. India is the key member in this regard and therefore had to take the lead in Meteorological Sector to provide infrastructure and technical know-how. Indian meteorological centre has provided atmospheric data to the members of the SAARC. This RMRC has served Bangladesh, India and Sri Lanka, particularly in forecasting cyclonic disasters. India is providing training to the scientists and technicians of SAARC member states in weather predictions. Thus India is serving other SAARC countries with technical collaboration in remote sensing and weather forecasting.[1]

India organised the first ever South Asian Annual Disaster Management Exercise(SAADMEx) from 23-26th November 2015 in New Delhi to provide participants with a practical, realistic exercise to address the diverse strategic issues of a multi-national disaster relief operation and coordination.[2]

4.3.6 Food Technology

The SAARC region is rich in agriculture products and forestry. Raw materials for processed food products are available from farms as well as forests. Food Technology is the new concept inducted in the SAARC region to have the finished goods in the agricultural and forestry sectors. The latest food technology is related to livestock preparation.

India played a dominant role in offering technical know-how in food technology to member states .of SAARC. India has also offered multi-location trials of Potatoes to the scientist members of SAARC. India's guidance for multi-location trials of ground nut, meetings on

1. Ghosh, A and P Sen (2012) Privatisation in a Small Open Economy with Imperfect Competition,Journal of Public Economic Theory, 14, 3, 441-71.
2. MEA, Government of India, 'SAARC Member Countries assemble to discuss preparations for the First South Asian Annual Disaster Management Exercise (SAADMEx) to be held in November 2015' Online Available at: https://mea.gov.in/outoging-visit-detail.htm?25788/SAARC+Member+Countries+assemble+to+discuss+preparations+for+the+First+South+Asian+Annual+Disaster+Management+Exercise+SAADMEx+to+be+held+in+November+2015

plant exploration and related activities etc., were proposed by India in the meetings of the technical committee on Agriculture and forestry. The technical know-how borrowed from India by other members of SAARC is being utilised for establishing their small and cottage industries, i.e. bakeries, tinned food, honey, wafers, cashew nuts etc.

4.3.6.1 SAARC Food Bank

Based on the decisions taken at the 14th SAARC Summit held in New Delhi on April 3-4, 2007, the leaders of the South Asian Association for Regional Cooperation (SAARC) signed an agreement to establish the SAARC Food Bank. Food banks complement national efforts to ensure food security for local people. The President approved the agreement establishing the SAARC Food Bank of India on April 17 2007.

India's initial valuation share in reserves was 1, 53,200 tonnes out of a total share of 2,43,000 tonnes. The estimated stock is currently held as 3,06,400 MT out of 4,86,000 MT. Stocks are stored at various strategic locations in designated Godowns of the Food Corporation of India (FCI). A Joint Chief (I.C.) of the Department of Food and Public Distribution has been nominated as a member of the Board of Directors of the SAARC Food Bank representing India. The Board considered and approved the proposal to designate the Central Grain Analysis Laboratory (CGAL), New Delhi, as the Regional Reference Laboratory for the SAARC Food Bank.

The 9th meeting of the SAARC Food Bank Board (SFB) was held on 21-22 September 2016 in Kathmandu, Nepal. As a member of the Board of Directors of SAARC Food Bank, India represented the meeting at the level of Joint Secretary (IC) of the sector. The meeting discussed, among other things, the issues related to the review of the implementation of the decisions taken at the eighth meeting of the SAARC Food Banks Board and the amendments to the agreement related to the establishment of the SAARC Food Banks. The topic discussed was strengthening food security in the region through collaboration and cooperation with banks and international organisations (FAO, IFAD, WFP, etc.). A presentation was also made by the SAARC Agriculture Center on the status of the SAARC Food Bank Information System (SFBIS).

Regional food security is an area where India can take great forward-looking initiatives and can be a major facilitator.[1]

1. SAARC Food Bank, Department of Food and Public Distribution, Government of India, Online Available at: https://dfpd.gov.in/saarc-food-bank.htm

4.3.7 Cultural Sector

India has been extending financial support to a number of cultural organisations working for regional integration in the SAARC context. SAARC Bands Festival, Literature Festival and Crafts Festivals, and Folklore Festivals have become annual features. A SAARC Museum of Textiles and Handicrafts and Training Centre is being established in New Delhi.

4.3.8 Environment Sector

The environment was included in the SAARC programme, but it drew urgent attention in 1997. The Heads of State or Government of the SAARC member states decided to appoint a commission to study "Causes and consequences of natural disaster and protection or preservation of the environment". Later on, the regional study, which was completed in 1991, was approved, and the committee on the environment was established in February 1992. This committee was responsible for studyinghe the environmental problems, causes and measures to overcome tovercomehese causes. The recommendation of the regional study was as follows: Taking immediate action to identify the problematic area of the environment, measures for strengthening the environment management infrastructure; a SAARC forestry and watershed programme, programme on energy and environment pollution control and hazardous waste management programme; programme on environmental sound, land and water use planning research and action programme on mountain development in Himalaya region; coastal zone management programme for bio-diversity management, information exchange on low cost and environmental sound habitat technologies, the establishment of a SAARC relief and assistance; a mechanism for disaster and regional cooperation on the development of modem disaster warning system.

India and Bangladesh are the worst affected nations among the SAARC members. Pollution of water is a grave problem in these countries. Cleaning rivers and freeing them from pollution is a problem yet to be undertaken on a large scale. Water pollution is health hazardous to the natives of these states. Air pollution is primarily restricted to the industrialised, urbanised pockets of India, Pakistan, Bangladesh and Sri Lanka. India is the worst affected among these, and therefore environmental study, particularly related to air. U water pollution is given providence in the action plan of India. In other areas, measures are taken to keep atmosphere and water resources free from pollution, but the measures taken are inadequate. Therefore, India, along with all other members of the SAARC, is working to free the south Asia Region from air and water pollution through their cooperative movement.

India understands and appreciates the concern over the challenge of climate change in the region. It has established an Endowment for Climate Change corpus of Rs. 25 crores to finance environment-related projects. South Asian countries can benefit from India's eco-blueprint by focusing on the **protection of biodiversity** and responding to the climate crisis. The linkage between **effective governance and sustainable development** also needs to be acknowledged in South Asian countries.

Information Sector

SAARC is established for the development of the South Asia Region. The core of development is always information; therefore, information science acquires the utmost importance. The committee related to it becomes a prominent committee to contribute its share in Region Development Programme. The standing committee decided that the documentation expert committee should initiate action and its first meeting for the establishment of a data bank on economic and social indicators of member countries and involve, for this purpose, a standard format for information.

India is using a geostationary communication satellite as a communication network to cover all the countries of the region for the transfer of data on land surveys and information on agricultural resources of the region. India's Remote sensing satellite is in the service of the countries of the region. The Regional Centre for Science and Technology of the SAARC will act as an agent to make adequate information available to the member states, whoever makes a request for it.

A regional information centre which will act as an information bank is created. This bank is making of I neuters for the storage of information. The present format of information kept in the form of textbooks and journals is outdated. Certain technologies have security and defence implications, so information transfer is allowed only in restricted areas.

Certain areas were chosen by the study group of the seven South Asian countries. The Science and Technology study group identified the priority areas for cooperation among the South Asian Regional Countries. They are discussed in the subchapters of this Chapter. The role played by India in establishing and working these committees is explained thereby. India is the only state in the South Asian Region which has the capability to lead the development of the South Asia Region in a short period if some of the member countries, out of jealousy towards India, do not hinder the work carried out by it in respect of the progress of the South Asian Region.[1]

India has also called for a Regional Air Services Agreement and offered to help in creating an enabling environment to reduce telecommunications costs to improve connectivity.

4.3.9.1 South Asian Satellite (Formerly SAARC Satellite)

India's successful launch of South Asia's first satellite (SAS) has boosted connectivity among six neighbouring countries and improved connectivity in times of disaster, opening a "new horizon of engagement" in the region. A unique position in space diplomacy Prime Minister Modi envisioned the 2,230-kilogram communications spacecraft as India's "precious gift" to neighbouring countries, sending a message that the "unprecedented" development "isn't even the sky's limit when it comes to regional cooperation." Built by the Indian Space Research Organization (ISRO) and fully funded by India, GSAT-9 will be launched from the Sriharikota spaceport off the coast of Andhra Pradesh on a GSLV-F09 rocket.[2]

Known as India's technology powerhouse, the satellite will help drive progress across the region, from the skies to the people of the region. It is also expected that relations between Afghanistan, Bangladesh, Bhutan, India, Maldives, Nepal and Sri Lanka will be strengthened. Successful launch of ISRO with a video conference with Prime Minister Modi, President Ashraf Ghani of Afghanistan, Prime Minister Sheikh Hasina of Bangladesh, Prime Minister Thring Tobgi of Bhutan, President Abdullah Yameen of Maldives, Prime Minister Pushpa Kamal Dahal of Nepal and President Maithripala The Sri Lankan Senate jointly celebrated.

Pakistan is not a part of the project as it had refused to accept India's "invaluable gift", proposed by Modi soon after he became the Prime Minister in 2014. The initial proposal to name it "SAARC Satellite" was

---

1. Moazzem, K. G. 2012. Foreign Direct Investment (FDI) in Bangladesh (1972–2010): An Exploratory Note from the Host Country Perspective. In Bangladesh at 40: Changes and Challenges. Dhaka: Academic Publishers.
2. PIB, Government of India, 'South Asian Satellite to boost regional communication' Online Retrieved From: https://pib.gov.in/newsite/printrelease.aspx?relid=161611

changed to South Asia Satellite following Pakistan's refusal. The satellite's footprint, extending all over South Asia, is for use by neighbours.

Globally, the gift has perhaps no precedent. The 2,230-kg communication spacecraft, with a mission life of 12 years, will support effective communication, broadcasting and Internet services in a region that is geographically challenging and economically lagging with limited technological resources. The SAS or GSAT-9 is a geosynchronous communications and meteorology satellite. It will provide a significant capability to each of the participating countries in terms of DTH (direct-to-home), besides linking the countries for disaster information transfer. It will help them with better governance, better banking and education in remote areas, more predictable weather forecasting and efficient natural resource mapping, linking people with top-end medical services through telemedicine and quick response to natural disasters. Its benefits also include deeper I.T. connectivity and fostering people-to-people contact.

Modi's view was shared by leaders of six other countries in South Asia, and they hailed India's gesture as a new face of cooperation in space for the common good of the neighbourhood. In his remarks, Ashraf Ghani noted that South Asia was one of the least integrated regions in the world. "South Asia today has taken a giant step towards regional integration...If cooperation through the land is impossible, we can connect through space."

Sheikh Hasina said the new satellite would change the face of South Asia and expand connectivity from land and water to space.

Tshering Tobgay described the launch as an "impressive milestone in the history of the world", with one country launching a satellite for the "free use of its neighbours".

Abdulla Yameen Abdul Gayoom said it underlined India's "neighbourhood first" foreign policy and showed its commitment to the development of the region. Asia becoming self-reliant in space science would boost connectivity in the region that, in turn, would spur development. Pushpa Kamal Dahal said the satellite was a "testimony" to the South.

Maithripala Sirisena said the satellite would help alleviate poverty and improve the living standards of South Asians.

War-ravaged Afghanistan alone does not share a border with India. Its Prime Minister Ashraf Ghani said, "If cooperation through the land is not possible, we can be connected through space."

The project cost India nearly RS 450 crore, with the satellite costing Rs 235 crore. This was GSLV's 11th launch. The SAS is orbiting the Earth in its Geosynchronous Transfer Orbit (GTO). In the coming days, the satellite orbit will be raised to the final circular Geostationary Orbit (GSO) by firing the satellite's Liquid Apogee Motor (LAM) in stages. It will be commissioned into service after the completion of orbit-raising operations and the satellite's positioning in its designated slot in the GSO following in-orbit testing of its payloads.[1]

4.3.10 Health Sector

In fulfilment of the announcements made by Prime Minister Modi at the XVIII SAARC Summit, (i) India has contributed US$ 1.05 million for the upgradation of the SAARC Tuberculosis, and HIV/AIDS Centre laboratory in Kathmandu to a supranational laboratory, (ii) A delegation from Afghanistan visited India in November 2015 to participate in the polio immunisation drive and learn from our best practices. The telemedicine project in Afghanistan offered by India is running successfully. The regime of Indian medical visas has been liberalised for SAARC nationals.[2] India is taking many steps to combat COVID-19 and providing Vaccines and Medicines to the member states.

4.3.10.1 India's Role and Initiatives to limit the outbreak of COVID-19 *in SAARC Regions*

India's engagement in the global humanitarian space has a long history, from initiatives in the Group of 77 and Non-Aligned Movement during the cold war to its extensive contemporary contribution to U.N. peacekeeping forces. India uses its region as the primary point of humanitarian departure, and the country's ability to project itself to regional and international audiences as a humanitarian actor and its interest in doing so are visible in South Asia.[3] Also, In recent years, India has been positioning itself as a "first responder" in regional humanitarian crises and taking a leadership role in managing emergencies under its "Neighbourhood

1 Ibid

2. Anil Trigunayat, (2017) India and the SAARC: Implications for the neighbourhood, MEA, Government of India. Online Retrieved From https://www.mea.gov.in/distinguished-lectures-detail.htm?655.

3. Vivekanandan, Jayashree, & Miklian, Jason. (2016) *'Bringing the region back in? ; Deciphering India's engagement with South Asia'*. NOREF Report, The Norwegian Peacebuilding Resource Centre.Available from: https://www.files.ethz.ch/isn/195946/95c1cff7e24a7a923ea51ad89a5d9e02.pdf (Accessed on March 30, 2020)

First" policy. In 2015, when a tragic earthquake of 7.9 magnitudes struck neighbouring Nepal, India was the first to send relief teams and aid. India has also been the first responder in other crises that have struck Indian Ocean littorals and islands. In 2017, India was the first to respond to the devastating Cyclone More that hit Sri Lanka and Bangladesh[1]. Now in this COVID-19 crisis, India's initiative towards SAARC countries is an outstanding example of its 'Neighbourhood first policy. The following are the Initiatives taken by India to limit the outbreak of COVID-19 in SAARC Regions.

- Before the SAARC videoconference, India had dispatched a 14-member medical team from its defence forces, including doctors and paramedics, to the Maldives to assist in fighting the pandemic. This initiative is important as perhaps this is the first-ever Indian medical team to go to another country.[2] Also, India evacuated more than 50 citizens from other countries, including Maldives, Myanmar, Bangladesh, China, the U.S., Madagascar, Sri Lanka, Nepal, South Africa and Peru, amid its own evacuations in the light of the COVID-19 outbreak.[3]
- **SAARC COVID-19 emergency fund**

During the virtual conference, Prime Minister Modi proposed to set up a COVID-19 emergency fund for SAARC countries on a voluntary basis. India will initially contribute $10 million, and it also announced that it would be putting together a team of specialists for the SAARC states. The fund has been operationalised, and the requirements of urgent medical supplies and equipment in individual countries are being met through this fund. Subsequently, Nepal and Afghanistan pledged $1 million each, Maldives committed $ 200,000, Bhutan $100,000, Bangladesh $1.5 million, Sri Lanka pledged $5 million to the

1. Home, K (March 23, 2020), *'COVID-19 crisis and SAARC diplomacy'*, Observer Research Foundation, Available from: https://www.orfonline.org/expert-speak/covid-19-crisis-and-saarc-diplomacy-63598/ (Accessed on April 10, 2020)
2. India Today(March 14, 2020) 'Coronavirus: Indian defence medical team in the Maldives to help deal with pandemic' Available from: https://www.indiatoday.in/india/story/coronavirus-indian-defence-medical-team-in-maldives-to-help-deal-with-pandemic-1655369-2020-03-14 (Accessed on April 20, 2020)
3. Panda, A (2020). "India Evacuates Citizens, Others from China, Iran Amid COVID-19". *The Diplomat.* March 10, 2020. Available From: https://thediplomat.com/2020/03/india-evacuates-citizens-others-from-china-iran-amid-covid-19/ (Accessed April 20, 2020)

fund, and **Pakistan** is the last member pledged $3 million to covid-19 Emergency Fund on the condition that the SAARC secretariat manages the fund.[1]. After Pakistan's Contribution total amount to the COVID-19 Emergency Fund is USD 21.8million. On its part, New Delhi has supplied various medical supplies, testing equipment and sanitisers, among other items, to Maldives, Afghanistan, Nepal, Bangladesh and Sri Lanka. These supplies were made through the release of one million dollars from a 10 million dollar allotment by India. Respective Indian Embassies coordinated the supplies under the guidance of Foreign Secretary Harsh Shringla following consultations with local governments.[2].

- The SAARC Disaster Management Centre setup consolidates India's role as a first responder in crises. It furthers 'Sabka Saath Sabka Vikas' policy in an external environment, especially in the neighbourhood.[3] Now in this critical juncture, Prime Minister Narendra Modi suggested that existing mechanisms like SAARC Disaster Management Centre can be used to pool best practices and create a common research platform to coordinate research on controlling epidemic diseases within the South Asian region. After this Suggestion, SAARC Disaster Management Centre (SDMC-IU), Gandhinagar, has set up a website (http://www.covid19-sdmc.org/) on COVID-19 for shared use of SAARC countries. The website shows the number of coronavirus cases in the member states and updates the numbers regularly. With the active participation of all member countries, the website aims to disseminate reliable information and updates on the evolving situation relating to COVID-19 in the region and best practices being followed in member countries. India believes that sharing

1 India Today (April 10, 2020), *'Pakistan pledges $3 million to SAARC Covid-19 Emergency Fund'* Available from: https://www.indiatoday.in/world/story/pakistan-pledges-3-million-saarc-covid19-emergency-fund-1665266-2020-04-10 (Accessed on April, 16,2020)

2. The Economic Times (March 20, 2020) *"India extends Covid assistance worth $ 1 million under SAARC emergency fund"* Available from: https://economictimes.indiatimes.com/news/politics-and-nation/india-extends-covid-assistance-worth-1-million-under-saarc-emergency fund/articleshow/74722067.cms?from=mdr (Accessed on April 12, 2020)

3 MEA, Government of India, (2017) *'Inauguration of SAARC Disaster Management Centre'* Available from: https://mea.gov.in/pressreleases.htm?dtl/28482/Inauguration_of_SAARC_Disaster_Management_Centre (Accessed on April 10, 2020)

resources, expertise, best practices and capacities in these challenging times would go a long way in bringing the countries in the SAARC region closer together, according to the MEA statement.[1].

- A SAARC meeting of health experts was held on March 26, 2020, and according to the Indian authorities which chaired the event, 'the enthusiastic and constructive participation by all SAARC member states demonstrated the shared commitment to work together to defeat the challenge posed by the coronavirus epidemic in the region.'[2] And all member States agreed that India would Share online training tools for emergency response teams and set up an Integrated Disease Surveillance Portal to help neighbouring countries trace and manage the coronavirus outbreaks within the South Asian region.[3]. As the follow-up action of the meeting, the All India Institute of Medical Sciences (AIIMS) in Raipur conducted four webinars on "COVID-19 Pandemic: Prevention and Management Guidelines" for the healthcare professionals of the SAARC nations. The Post Graduate Institute of Medical Education and Research in Chandigarh and the AIIMS in Bhubaneshwar will conduct webinars on other aspects related to responding to the pandemic in the coming days. Again Pakistan has stayed away from this training.[4]
- On April 8, 2020, India's led senior SAARC commerce officials hosted a call on the impact of coronavirus on regional trade. The

---

1. The Economic Times (March 23, 2020) *'SAARC health professionals meet on March 26 via video conference to contain Covid-19* 'Available from: https://economictimes.indiatimes.com/news/politics-and-nation/saarc-health-professionals-meet-on-mar-26-via-video-conference-to-contain-covid-19/articleshow/74779710.cms?from=mdr(Accessed on April 12, 2020)
2. Casaca, Paulo (2020), *'The virus and the SAARC's awakening'*, SADF COMMENT Issue no. 174, Available from: https://www.sadf.eu/comment-174-the-virus-and-the-saarcs- awakening/ (Accessed on April 11, 2020)
3. MEA, Government of India, (March 27, 2020) *'Video Conference of senior health professionals of SAARC countries on the fight against Covid-19'* Available from: https://mea.gov.in/pressreleases.htm?dtl/32603/Video_Conference_of_senior_health_professionals_of_SAARC_countries_on_the_fight_against_Covid19 (Accessed on April,10,2020)
4. The Deccan Herald (April 17, 2020), *'Pakistan again boycotts India's COVID-19 training programme for SAARC healthcare professionals,"* Available from: https://www.deccanherald.com/international/pakistan-again-boycotts-indias-covid-19-training-programme-for-saarc-healthcare-professionals-826657.html (Accessed on April 20, 2020)

discussion highlighted practical ways that all member states can continue to keep trade and transit relations open using regional frameworks. But Pakistan did not participate, saying such a meeting could only be effective if spearheaded by the SAARC secretariat instead of India. The Trade officials broadly agreed to identify new ways to 'sustain and expand' the intra-regional trade to offset the huge economic cost of the coronavirus pandemic. The meeting took place as a follow-up to an Indian-initiated video conference of SAARC leaders on March 15[1].

- Among other initiatives, the Indian government provided large consignments of hydroxychloroquine and paracetamol tablets and 5,000 tonnes of wheat to Afghanistan as an aid during the Covid-19 pandemic.[2]. The government of India has also donated 23 tonnes of essential medicines to Nepal to fight the COVID-19 pandemic. The consignment includes 8.25 lakhs dosage of essential medicines, including 3.2 lakhs dosage of Paracetamol and 2.5 lakhs dosages of Hydroxychloroquine.[3]. A 'special cell' in the Ministry of External Affairs of India is coordinating and monitoring the coordination of regional efforts with SAARC countries. The Indian Council of Medical Research (ICMR) also assists help in this health crisis. However, India believes that sharing resources, expertise, best practices and capacities in these challenging times would bring the countries in the SAARC region closer together.

These Initiatives taken by India have been praised by many International Organisations like WHO, World Bank etc. Many foreign nations also praised India for its role in SAARC regions in this critical situation. However, according to a European

1. India Today (April 9, 2020), *"Pakistan boycotts India-led meeting of SAARC trade officials on coronavirus crisis'* Available from: **https://www.indiatoday.in/world/story/pakistan-boycotts-india-led-meeting-saarc trade officials-coronavirus-crisis-1664904-2020-04-09**, (Accessed on April 13, 2020)
2. The Hindustan Times (April 20, 2020), *'Afghan Prez Ghani thanks India for supplying HCQ, wheat amid Covid-19 pandemic'* Available from: **https://www.hindustantimes.com/india-news/afghan-prez-ghani-thanks-india-for-supplying-hydroxychloroquine-wheat-amid-covid-19-pandemic/story s9iZwJGGwRQD2EdbGysF0N.html** (Accessed on April 21, 2020)
3. The Himalayan Times (April 22, 2020), *'India donates 23 tonnes of essential medicines to Nepal to fight Covid 19'* Available from: https://thehimalayantimes.com/kathmandu/india-donates-23-tonnes-of-essential-medicines-to-nepal-to-fight-covid-19/ (Accessed on April 23, 2020)

think-tank, the European Foundation For South Asian Studies (EFSAS), 'the regional leadership undertaken by New Delhi helped South Asia to contain the pandemic so far, and the pro-active strategy adopted by India and the rest of South Asia in tackling Covid-19, at least the total number of Covid-19 positive cases in South Asia is relatively low when compared to the close to a million reported in Europe and about 700,000 in the U.S. as of April 15.'[1].

The whole world is witnessing that during this COVID-19 crisis, India's cooperation with SAARC countries. India's successful attempt to bring the eight countries together through Prime Minister Narendra Modi's innovative idea to hold a video conference between the SAARC leaders to fight against Corona Crisis and the positive response it has received from SAARC member-states has helped the region prepare itself better in countering the pandemic that demands urgency and region-wide response. The regional leadership undertaken by India's Prime Minister, Shri Narendra Modi, helped South Asia to contain the pandemic. The SAARC countries have recorded much lower infection rates in the region compared to the worst affected countries, including the U.S., Western Europe and China. But irresponsible behaviour by Pakistan in the region could have a cascading effect on the whole of South Asia. As usual, India's leadership in SAARC is constantly challenged by Pakistan. Pakistan should realise that the future of the region lies in cooperation with India, and conflict and tension cannot take the country ahead. However, the crisis brought on by Covid-19 stresses the importance of deeper regional cooperation in South Asia. Countries in this region need to comprehend this need and make sincere efforts to put aside their differences which forbid such cooperation. The global crisis is an opportunity to revive SAARC, which has been dormant for several years.

4.3.11 Other Contributions

- The fledgling SAARC Development Fund (SDF) finances sub-regional projects envisaged under its social, economic and infrastructure windows. India is the only country to have paid its assessed contribution (for the entire 5-year period) of US$ 89.9

1. The Times of India (April 18, 2020), *'India's leadership helped South Asia to contain coronavirus so far, says European think-tank,'* Available from: https://timesofindia.indiatimes.com/india/indias-leadership-helped-south-asia-to-containcoronavirus-so-far-says-european-think tank/article show/75218919.cms(Accessed on April 22, 2020)

million and a voluntary contribution of US$ 100 million. Two regional projects - on women's empowerment and maternal and child health care - under SDF are currently being implemented with technical assistance from India.

- India is the prime mover behind the proposed Motor Vehicles Agreement and the Railways Agreement.
- India is also actively engaged in the implementation of the SAARC Framework Agreement for Energy Cooperation which offers a conducive environment to facilitate cross-border electricity trade within the SAARC region.
- A currency swap arrangement for the region, with a base fund of US$ 2 billion from India, provides short-term foreign exchange liquidity requirements of Member States.
- India has also funded regional development projects in telemedicine, tele-education, rural solar electrification, rainwater harvesting, seed testing laboratories and shuttle breeding of pulses using a hub-and-spokes approach. The projects, in various stages of implementation, have been greatly appreciated by the recipient SAARC countries.
- India was the first country to reach out to Nepal in the aftermath of the devastating earthquake. Our emergency assistance drew appreciation from all quarters.
- India has hosted key SAARC Ministers of Transport, Home, Finance, Trade, Agriculture, Culture, Health, Environment, Education and Science & Technology meetings. It has organised a number of training programmes/workshops/seminars on subjects as diverse as space technology, performance management, and digital economy to tourism.
- India has also organised a number of workshops/seminars/ training programmes on disaster management for the SAARC member states.
- India is fully aware of the challenges in South Asia, with cross-border terrorism being the most serious. At the last Informal Meeting of SAARC Foreign Ministers held in New York on the sidelines of the U.N. General Assembly on September 26 2019, India stressed how the problems that beset SAARC were not just a story of missed opportunities but also of deliberate obstacles, terrorism is one of them. That elimination of terrorism in all its

forms is a precondition not only for fruitful cooperation but also for the very survival of our region itself.[1]

4.4 Obstacles to India's Initiatives in the SAARC

Individual states of the region matter to one another depending on their geography and politics. In the case of non-South Asian states, a South Asian state approaches them mostly in bilateral terms for economic and strategic reasons. China and America are the common denominators in this complex web of relationships. China's proximity to the region and its growing power makes it the most important factor. Since it has a strategic partnership with Pakistan and India-Pakistan relations are problematic, the China card comes in handy to most of India's neighbours to bargain with India. Bangladesh, Nepal, Sri Lanka, and even to some extent, Bhutan have played the China card and, at times, even the Pakistan card to neutralise India's predominance. The Maldives is the only exception, where Chinese interest so far is minimal.

India has undertaken moderate policy initiatives concerning SAARC activities and pursued an accommodative policy to inspire confidence among its neighbours to help fulfil SAARCs cherished goals. India has, however, not achieved the desired outcome in its endeavours. Being held hostage to factors such as India-Pakistan rivalry, mutual mistrust, and lack of requisite political will among leaders of South Asian countries, SAARC has got mired in confusion and uncertainty. This does not augur well for SAARC moving forward.

However, India's contribution to the SAARC is undoubtedly the driving force to strengthen the organisation. Still, India has been facing some obstacles regarding her initiatives in the SAARC. They are:

- The small neighbour countries of SAARC feel the "Big Brother Syndrome" about India. India's larger size of territory made India the most striking culprit in the eyes of its smaller neighbours in the SAARC.
- Due to its economic strength and scientific and technological development, India is creating suspicion of domination by India in the minds of smaller neighbours.
- Pakistan factor is another obstacle to India's initiative in SAARC. Although the two countries were the largest and accounted for

1. MEA, Government of India, ' India-SAARC" Online Available at: https://mea.gov.in/Portal/ForeignRelation/India_SAARC_2020. pdf

80% of SAARC's area, more than 85% of its population and more than 90% of its GDP, Pakistan's unbroken hostility has led to its initiative in SAARC. For example, India and a few SAARC members boycotted the 19th SAARC summit in Islamabad because of the Pakistan-sponsored terrorist attack on J&K's Uri military camp. And finally, it was shaved.

- China's intervention in South Asian countries is also one of the obstacles to India's initiative in SAARC. China is bordered by India, Pakistan, Nepal, Bhutan and Myanmar. Except for India, all are Least Developed Countries (LDCs). For this reason, China is increasing its influence in these countries by investing billions of dollars and providing subsidised loans. Undoubtedly, this will lead to curbing India's influence in the South Asian region.
- Another obstacle facing India's initiative in SAARC is that smaller SAARC members like Bangladesh, Nepal and Sri Lanka see India as a major threat to their security. They directly or indirectly welcomed the role of regional extraterritorial powers in countering India's military might and alleged military threats.

India should take these steps to overcome the above obstacles regarding India's initiatives in the SAARC. Firstly, India should change its policies and attitudes towards its neighbours as the smaller members of SAARC claim to show big brotherhood. India should implement the Gujral doctrine more effectively than ever in this context. Secondly, it is the need of the hour for India to be more generous to its neighbours in areas such as infrastructure, energy, water, trade, climate change mitigation, higher education, healthcare and military cooperation, which should improve among the neighbour countries of India. Thirdly, India should curb China's interference in the South Asian region by applying democratic principles and non-neocolonialism and promoting trust in its neighbours. Because China has adopted a communist dictatorial policy at home and an exploitative trade policy abroad, both of which are signs of autocratic rule and neo-colonialism. Finally, in order to improve India's initiative in SAARC, India should act as the guardian of SAARC in relation to its objectives and implementation. India should play a double role in this regard. On the one hand, it includes China's intervention in the South Asian region, and on the other, it promotes Pakistan's presence in SAARC activities. Unless India follows these policies perfectly, her initiatives should not be materialised in the SAARC.

Chapter - 5

Conclusion

The present study attempted to inquire into various aspects of regional cooperation in South Asia in the preceding chapters with the objective of gaining a meaningful understanding of SAARC as a phenomenon. This study started with an essential conceptual discussion on regions, South Asia as a viable region and proceeded to study the evolution and genesis of SAARC as a regional organization of South Asia. The socio-economic and political dimensions of the region's states, their internal problems, their bilateral relations, the role of India and its contributions to SAARC have been discussed in detail. An evaluation of the functioning of SAARC and India's initiatives for the progress of SAARC during these years has also been undertaken.

The study started with a conceptual discussion about the South Asian region. It indicates that there were strong factors in South Asia, like the geography, proximity, history, society, security perception and nation-building process etc., commonalities in the social and cultural aspects and economic background. These factors and interference of the big powers, in some way or another, paved the path for the regional organization in South Asia

The genesis of SAARC is also one of them. The origin of SAARC in its present form could be traced to the proposals mooted by the late President Zia-ur-Rehman of Bangladesh in 1980, followed by the circulation of the Working Paper on South Asian Regional Cooperation in November 1980. The formal discussions for the establishment of an institutional mechanism for regional cooperation in South Asia started with the Colombo meeting of the Foreign Secretaries of the seven states of the South Asian region, i.e. Bangladesh, Bhutan, India, Maldives, Nepal, Pakistan and Sri Lanka in April 1981.

The evolution of regional organizations in South Asia has indeed been very late in comparison to various other regions of the world, including other Asian regions. There were several reasons, but the most important among them were India and Pakistan. As the study indicates, the turning point in the evolution of regional cooperation in South Asia was the New Delhi Meeting of Foreign Ministers in August 1983, where an embryonic form of regional cooperation, viz. South Asian Regional Cooperation (SARC) was launched. After a few more meetings at the Foreign Ministers' level, the formal launching of SAARC in its present form took place in Dhaka in December 1985. The Dhaka Summit of the SAARC (South Asian Association for Regional Cooperation) Heads of State or Governments adopted the Charter of the SAARC. It marked the beginning of regional cooperation. Afghanistan joined as the 8th member of SAARC in 2007.

The SAARC Charter reaffirmed the conviction of the member states about the necessity and desirability of regional cooperation and declared that SAARC was intended to 'promote the welfare of the people of South Asia and to improve their quality of life, to accelerate economic growth, social progress and cultural development in the region…and to promote and strengthen collective self-reliance among the countries of South Asia.'[1]. The Charter also enunciated that cooperation within the framework of SAARC should be based on 'respect for the principles of sovereign equality, territorial integrity, political independence, non-interference in internal affairs of other States and mutual benefit. The tenets of Non-Alignment and the UN were also affirmed as the guiding forces of SAARC.

Another theme of the work is the influence of the major external powers, i.e. the United Kingdom, United States, Soviet Union and China, on the intra-regional relations of South Asia and the prospects of regional cooperation. It has been attempted to analyze how these major powers affected the South Asian region and the South Asian states. The relations between India, the core of the South Asian region and its neighbours, particularly Pakistan, Nepal, Sri Lanka and Bangladesh, have been affected adversely by the involvement of these major powers in the region.

The study also indicates that the countries of South Asia are characterized by eternal internal turmoil and problems of political stability

1. E. Sudhakar, SAARC Origin, Growth and Future, Gyan Publishing House, New Delhi, 1994, p. 190.

and national integration. All the states have been facing this problem for the past few decades. Moreover, the social, cultural, ethnic and religious affiliations of the people of the region transcending national boundaries created a crisis of confidence and distrust. It is a common feature of the region that each state gates its neighbour states for internal troubles. These intra-regional and inter-regional conflicts have also been discussed in the study.

The study also examined the Indo-Centric nature of the South Asian region, India's efforts and initiatives towards regional cooperation, its bilateral issues with the neighbouring countries and India's contributions to SAARC. Most of the states of the region over the past decades developed an adversary relationship with India. The basis for this is partly the bilateral problems they have with India, and partly it is psychological. This negative relationship between the states of South Asia with India gives rise to small states' tendency and their fear of big Nations. India is the largest of all the member states of South Asia. Most of the bilateral issues revolve around India and other member states.

India-Pakistan bilateral relations occupy the centre stage of South Asian relations. The major bilateral problems are India's problems of Kashmir with Pakistan, river water disputes with Nepal, smuggling and sharing river waters problems with Bangladesh, and Tamil insurgency with Sri Lanka. These problems are purely bilateral, and no other South Asian country plays any role. India also played a positive role in SAARC by encouraging cooperation among the South Asian states. It has good relations with Maldives and Bhutan and cordial relations with other South Asian states regarding economic cooperation.

The study also highlights SAARC's comparison with other Regional organizations like ASEAN and EU. SAARC though a latecomer on the international scene, has been quite ahead of other regional organizations like ASEAN in the institutional framework. But the institutional mechanism established by SAARC is relatively modest compared to other similar organizations. While comparing SAARC with other regional organizations, it is found that, in most cases, political, social and ideological convergence facilitated their evolution. In the case of SAARC, in spite of the existence of social, cultural and ethnic commonalities, the strategic and ideological divergence stemming from religious variation and antagonistic political postures are found to be causing most of the damage to the unity of the region. However, the evolution of SAARC indicates the desire of the countries of South Asia to bring about unity to realize regional cooperation. By analyzing the above discussion, this can be said that there is no problem with the general framework of regionalism as far as SAARC is concerned. SAARC is quite an in-order regional organization in South Asia. Its need was felt for quite a long time, and its emergence took longer than other similar regional organizations. SAARC, with its noble objectives, is compatible with the ideals and objectives of the United Nations and the Non-Aligned Movement.

The commitment of the members of SAARC to its a vowed objectives of cooperation, peace, progress, prosperity and stability of the region sometimes vacillates. It is pretty challenging to say that they are committed to their a vowed objectives as India and Pakistan's mutual rivalries are still unresolved. It has been mentioned in SAARC's objectives that no bilateral issues would be discussed in SAARC summits. But still, SAARC summits cannot spare themselves from such discussion. SAARC summits were often postponed due to tensions between these two major powers.

There is mutual suspicion among the member states of SAARC. It was especially questioned how far Indian hegemonism in South Asia is real and how it affects Regional Cooperation in South Asia. It is quite true that the fundamental reality of the size and strength of India in relation to its neighbours gave scope for this kind of suspicion in the bilateral relations between India and its neighbours. The mutual suspicions in the bilateral relations have their roots in social, cultural, religious, ethnic and political factors. The suspicions were rather psychological and by no means impossible. Once they are removed, there will be closer interaction between India and its neighbours both at the state and state levels.

The talk of Indian hegemonism or Indophobia has its roots in the bilateral problems between India and its neighbours. India's ambitious foreign policy postures and insistence on bilateralism in dealing with its smaller neighbours are construed as dominant aspirations.[1] But the fact is that India is generally keen on maintaining good neighbourly relations with all its smaller neighbours. India has been more interested in economic relations with its smaller neighbours. The problem of India's big size is an actual and imaginary problem fostered by Pakistan for obvious reasons and actively supported by external powers, particularly the USA and China. The talk of India's big size is, in a way, an assertion of identity by the

1. Leo O. Rose, India's Regional Policy: Non-military Dimensions' in Stephen P. Cohen, The Security of South Asia, Vistara, New Delhi, 1987, p. 4.

smaller states of South Asia. This way, they were more or less successful in wresting quite a few concessions from India apart from isolating it both within the region as well as SAARC.

As far as the influence of major powers is concerned. It is true that the world's major powers, like US, Russia and China, have a definite influence on SAARC. They were in some way or other responsible for the emergence of a feeling of regional cooperation among the South Asian states.

A few problems can be quickly resolved through political will and a change in mindset. The issue includes the bilateral relations between the member states, their internal problems, religious diversities, anti-Indian attitude of the South Asian states, Indian-Pakistan rivalries and the major power interference and their effect on the regional evaporation in south Asia.

The above-mentioned problems of SAARC are not such they cannot be resolved; if SAARC members think positively and behave patiently, there will be hope for its end. An objective and open-minded approach will clear the misunderstandings and mutual distrust in bilateral relations among India and other South Asian states. A strong political will and a spirit of accommodation based on giving and taking will not only solve all the bilateral problems among these states but also pave the way for the progress of regional cooperation.

The internal problems or turmoil in various states of South Asia is a major factor in fomenting troubles in the bilateral relations of these countries. Most of the problems are systematic oriented and can be solved by introducing necessary changes and confidence-building measures.

Another factor influencing the progress of SAARC is small states' tendency and suspicion about India. Something has to be done by all the member states of SAARC to remove this dubious phenomenon which has created a lot of bad blood in the intra-regional politics of South Asia. As the problem is centred on India, India needs to make some efforts as discussed and proposed in Gujral Doctrine.

India needs to adopt a more accommodative approach to resolving the issues with its neighbours. The issue includes Kachchativu with Sri Lanka, some disputed territorial enclaves, Ganga waters, cross-border migration with Bangladesh, and issues pertaining to Mahakali and Kalapani with Nepal. It is encouraging that some issues have been settled. Gujral Doctrine'envisaged that India would go the extra mile to iron out differences with its neighbours. India has certainly adopted a positive approach and constantly engages in substantive dialogue with them. There is no substitute for dialogue. A composite dialogue to resolve all the differences with Pakistan, But Pakistan should stop terrorist activities against India. Nepal and Bangladesh though not very friendly, are free to take their stand on international issues they perceive. Sri Lanka also dealt with an economic issue without India's instruction. India will undoubtedly be happy if peace and stability return to this Indian Ocean Island.[1].

As far as smaller states are concerned, the establishment of SAARC has brought about sovereign equality among all the region states, irrespective of their size or strength. Hence, there is no scope for identity problems in the smaller states. Thus the smaller states of South Asia have to adjust to the reality of the core status of India in the region. Mutual trust and confidence among the smaller states on the one hand and India on the other is the only way out of this peculiar ailment of SAARC.

India-Pakistan bitter relations are also one of the major hurdles in the success of SAARC. The future of the SAARC is directly related to Indo-Pak relations. While India seems to have shown keen interest in bringing harmony to Indo-Pak relations, Pakistan has consistently tried to vitiate the chances of rapprochement.[2] Pakistan continues to harp on the Kashmir issue. It makes it an essential precondition for Indo-Pak normalization, while India considers Kashmir an integral part of India, and the issue is closed. Remedies for this problem are difficult to find, but they are not impossible. The past and present pattern of indo-Pak relations does not indicate any dramatic improvement. However, one can hope that saner counsel will prevail in the ruling elites of both states, especially in Pakistan, so that a sense of permanent peace could down on the Indian sub-continent heralding a bright future of economic prosperity and social and cultural harmony.

India has undertaken moderate policy initiatives concerning SAARC activities and pursued an accommodative policy to inspire confidence among its neighbours to help fulfil SAARCs cherished goals. India has, however, not achieved the desired outcome in its endeavours. Being held hostage to factors such as India-Pakistan rivalry, mutual mistrust, and lack of requisite political will among leaders of South Asian countries, SAARC

1. R.S. Siwach, "South Asia Heading Towards South Asian Union", South Asia Politics, Issue II, March 2004, pp. 47.
2. Indian Express, 1 Jul. 1992.

has got mired in confusion and uncertainty. This does not augur well for SAARC moving forward.

Although SAARC's dismal past Indian Prime Minister Modi has boldly stroked new hope for the future of SAARC. Modi is widely seen as a reformist prime minister expected to open up the economy and liberalize trade. In addition, agreements from visits to neighbouring countries reveal a particular line of thinking – cooperation, particularly in infrastructure and energy, targeted at resolving shared problems. It is, therefore, logical that the government would seek similar opportunities to expand and deepen the engagement with SAARC.[1]

However, In this COVID-19 Period, Perhaps for the first time, the baneful aphorism used in the context of SAARC, that South Asia is the "most disconnected region in the world", is seen as a respite in the light of the searing contagion that has brought the world to a screeching halt. But that crisis presents the region with an opportunity like never before. Even when a global crisis looms large, India has depicted that the SAARC spirit should be sustained, and the organizational platform can be used to foster regional cooperation.[2]

A stable South Asia benefits India, as India is the largest country in the region, so India's role becomes crucial. But other benefits cannot be done at the cost of internal security, sovereignty, and terrorism. But if India is seeking its role as a global leader, then India must stabilize the SAARC.

The success of SAARC will hinge on an enduring peace between the two major powers- India and Pakistan- in the region as well as the determination of the leaders to strengthen the SAARC in promoting shared regional interests. Member states need to look at the ugly reality that about 40 per cent of the people in the world living on less than a dollar a day belong to South Asia. In the face of the non-availability of even the basic amenities of life to a large chunk of the people, it becomes a moral responsibility of India, a giant member country, to boost goodwill and cooperation within the SAARC community. Regional socio-economic cooperation deserves top priority. Therefore, India has advocated such cooperation extending into regional economic integration to eliminate poverty, raise people's living

1. Sidhu, W.P.S & Sandhu Rohan. (2014) *"Reinvigorating SAARC India's Opportunities and Challenges"*, Brookings India.
2. Mishra Vivek, (2020), 'SAARC's Resurrection: Leadership in the Time of COVID-19' Indian Council for World Affairs, Online Retrieved From: https://www.icwa.in/show_content.php?lang=1&level=3&ls_id=4651&lid=3503

standards and usher in regional prosperity. India will continue to emphasize enhancing regional trade and cooperation and people-to-people contact. At the same time, by the logic of economic globalization and the consequent importance of economic strength in a national power calculus, India cannot be tied to the unmoving SAARC (living in the manifest from India's ever-deepening regional economic blocs such burgeoning bilateral trade with has no future without India. The role of India is inevitable if SAARC has to make any progress, but with a word of caution that India needs to act as a statesman to harmonize its neighbourhood policies while taking account of sensitivities and legitimate concerns and interests of smaller countries of the region. At the same time, India needs to demonstrate through its action that it will take appropriate steps and initiatives like providing more funds to address the region's socio-economic problems as well as stepping up confidence-building measures among member states with whom India has long-standing bilateral disputes.[1]

India's efforts to promote regionalism in South Asia through the aegis of 'SAARC continues to be marred by the importance of contentiousness. Politics among the nations of the region, particularly between India and Pakistan. The challenge before the Indian policy establishment, therefore, is daunting. Indian policy has to respond to the difficult task of smoothening the political and strategic divergence in the region. This is essential for the dynamism generated by the socio-economic cooperation under SAARC to acquire a decisive edge to make South Asian regionalism a success story.[2]

Without Indian initiative or interest in prioritizing a more inclusive South Asian multilateralism, we are unlikely to see South Asia cohere as a region over common concerns. Further, it is doubtful that SAARC will be able to emerge as a counter-veiling force to international pressures. The extent to which this will influence India's strategic ambitions remains uncertain. More apparent is that by employing bilateralism to satisfy national interest calculations, the Modi government continues along a foreign policy path in the region that is often more counterproductive than constructive. While it is simplistic to say that India assumes its mantle of South Asian hegemon by expecting deference from its neighbours, a more engaged, multilateral approach might make the country's neighbours feel

1. Jain, Romi. "India and SAARC: An Analysis." *Indian Journal of Asian Affairs*, vol. 18, no. 2, 2005, pp. 55–74. *JSTOR*, http://www.jstor.org/stable/41950459. Accessed 14 Oct. 2022.
2. Sharma, Suman. "INDIA AND SAARC." India Quarterly, vol. 57, no. 2, 2001, pp. 99–120. JSTOR, http://www.jstor.org/stable/45073261. Accessed 15 Oct. 2022.

more respected as equals. Crucially, it would provide new opportunities for India to offer inclusive leadership to help resolve some of South Asia's most vexing and intractable challenges.

India needs to change its current approach to maintain its regional position. India needs to set priorities which benefit smaller countries and give a big thrust to the SAARC movement. The current Prime Minister of India, Narendra Modi and his government's proactive focus is on India's foreign policy and has ushered in a new era of the India-SAARC relationship. India has changed its approach towards its neighbours; for India, now neighbours will be its priority.

However, the present study envisages a comprehensive observation of Indian efforts to maintain peace, security and stability in the SAARC region. It also comprehensively analyses India's engagement with SAARC member states. This research also includes the evolution and genesis of SAARC, the Indian attitude and performance, and its overall contribution to the development and achievement of SAARC.

Bibliography

Books:

1. Appadorai, A., and M.S. Rajan. (1988), '*India's Foreign Policy and Relations*', New Delhi, South Asia Publication.
2. Appadorai, A. (1988) '*Contemporary India: Essays in Domestic and Foreign Policy*', New Delhi, South Asia Publication.
3. Bailes and A. Wivel (2014), '*Small States and International Security: Europe and Beyond*', Abingdon ,Routledge
4. Banerjee, Dipankar, (ed.), (2002), '*SAARC in the Twenty-First Century: Towards a Cooperative Future*', New Delhi, Published by India Research Press.
5. Bhan, Pankaj, Srivastava, R.N. (2008), 'SAARC – *Evolutionary Cycle of Growth and Consolidation, in SAARC Socio-Economic Transformation Foundation for peace and sustainable development*', Delhi, D.K. Fine Art Press Pvt. Ltd.
6. Bhargava, K.K. and Khatri, Shridhar K. (eds). (2002), 'South *Asia 2010 Challenges and Opportunities*', Delhi, Konark Publishers.
7. Bose Anuradha (Das), (2011), *"SAARC A Quest for Unity: Problems and Prospects"*. Kolkata: Minerva Associates (Publications), In Association with Nabagram Hiralal Paul College, Political Science Department, Hoogly.
8. Chaudhary, Anasua Basu Ray, *'SAARC at Cross Roads, The Fate of Regional Cooperation in South Asia'*, New Delhi: Shivam Offset Press.
9. Dahl, Ann Sofie (1997), *"To Be or Not To Be Neutral: Swedish Security Strategy in the Post-Cold War Era*", in Efraim Inbar and Gabriel Sheffer (eds.) The National Security of Small States in a Changing World, Frank Cass Publishers: London/ Portland.
10. Dash, Kishore C. (2008), *"Regionalism in South Asia: Negotiating Cooperation, Institutional Structures"*: New Delhi, Routledge.
11. Dixit, J.N. (1999) '*Liberation and Beyond: Indo-Bangladesh Relations*, New Delhi, Konark Publishers.
12. Eric & Nancy, (eds). (1999), *"The Dynamics of South Asia Regional Cooperation and SAARC"*, New Delhi: Sage Publications.
13. Emajuddin Ahmed. (1985), *'SAARC: Seeds of Harmony'*, Dhaka, The University Press.
14. Emanual Nahar, Sheveta Sehgal, (2014), *'SAARC in Contemporary World: Issues and Concerns'*, New Delhi, Swastik Publications.

15. E. Sudhakar, (1994), '*SAARC Origin, Growth and Future*', Gyan Publishing House, New Delhi.
16. Garg, Jayanti Prasad. (1980), *'Regionalism in International Politics'*, New Delhi, Research Publication.
17. Gonasalves Eric and Jetly Nancy (eds.).(1999), '*The Dynamics of South Asia: Regional Cooperation and SAARC*', New Delhi, Sage Publication.
18. Gupta, Bhabani Sen (ed.) (1988), '*SAARC – ASEAN Prospects and Problems of Inter-Regional Cooperation*', New Delhi, South Asian Publishers.
19. Gupta, Bhabani Sen. (1988), *'South Asian Perspectives: Seven Nations in Conflicts and Co-Operation'*, New Delhi, B.R. Publication.
20. Goel, O.P. (2004), '*India and SAARC Engagement*', New Delhi, Isha Publication.
21. Hussain, M.M. (1980), '*Prospects and Problems in Cooperation among Small Nations in South Asia*', Colombo, Margo Institute.
22. Jain, B.M. (1985), '*South Asian Security: Problems and Prospects*', New Delhi, Radiant Publishers.
23. Jay, P.A., (1996), '*SAARC: Trade and Development*', New Delhi, Deep and Deep Publication.
24. Jetly, Nancy. (1989), 'Emergence of SAARC, in Bimal Prasad (ed.), *Regional Cooperation in South Asia: Problems and Prospects*, New Delhi, Vikas Publishing House.
25. Jain, B.N. (1985), '*South Asian Security Problems and Prospects*', New Delhi, Radiant Publication.
26. Joy, P.A. (1995) '*SAARC Trade and Development*', New Delhi, Deep & Deep Publications.
27. Karunkaran, K.P. (1954), '*India in World Affairs*', Delhi, Oxford University Press.
28. Katyal, G. and Bhushan K. (2002) '*SAARC Challenges before New Millennium*' New Delhi, A.P.H. Publishing Corporation.
29. Kher, R.S. (2004), *'SAARC: Political and Economic Aspects'*, New Delhi, Dominant Publishers and Distributors.
30. Kulwant Kaur and Baljit Singh Mann (eds.,) (2006), '*South Asia: Dynamics of Politics, Economy and Security*', New Delhi, Knowledge World Publication.
31. Maatli, W. (1999) *'the Logic of Regional Integration: Europe and Beyond'*. Cambridge: Cambridge University Press.
32. Madaan, Davinder Kumar.(1997) *'SAARC: Origin, Development and Programmes'*, New Delhi, Deep & Deep Publications.
33. Mahapatra, P.C., South Asian Economic Cooperation: Problems and Prospects, in Debendra K. Das (ed.), *SAARC: Regional Cooperation and Development*, New Delhi, Deep & Deep Publications, 1996.
34. Maniruzzaman, Talukder (1982), *'The Security of Small States in the Third World'*, the Australian National University: Canberra.
35. Mishra, Parmod Kumar. (1990) '*South-South Cooperation: A SAARC Perspective*', Calcutta, Chatterjee Publishers.

36. Moazzem, K. G. (2012) *'Foreign Direct Investment (FDI) in Bangladesh (1972–2010): An Exploratory Note from the Host Country Perspective. In Bangladesh at 40: Changes and Challenges'*. Dhaka: Academic Publishers.
37. Mohla, Vandana. (1998) '*SAARC and Super Powers'*, Deep & Deep Publication, New Delhi.
38. Nahar, Emmanuel.(1991) '*SAARC: Problems & Prospects'*, New Delhi, Sehgal Publication.
39. Panchmukhi, V.R. (1990), 'Economic *Cooperation in the SAARC Region: Potential Constraints and Policies'*, New Delhi, Research and Information System.
40. Pradhan, Bishma., (1989), '*SAARC and its Future'*, Delhi, Vikas Publishing House Pvt. Ltd.
41. Rehman, S.(1999). *'Regional Economic Cooperation in South Asia'*. In Ghosh, P.K. (Ed.), A Modernization Perspective (pp. 268- 271).London: Greenwood Press.
42. Sinha, Harsh Kumar, (1994), 'India's *Role in SAARC',* Delhi, Rahul Publishing House.
43. Sudhakar, E.(1994), '*SAARC – Origin, Growth and Future*', New Delhi, Gyan Publishing House.
44. Syed, M.H. (2002) 'Encyclopedia *of SAARC Nations*', Vol. I, Delhi, Kalpaz Publications.
45. Syed, M.H. (2002) *'Encyclopedia of SAARC*', Vol. II and Vol. III, Delhi, Kalpaz Publications.
46. Sridharan, K. (2010). *'SAARC and the Evolving Asian Regionalism. In S. Muni (Ed.), the Emerging Dimensions of SAARC'.*
47. Upreti, B.C. (2000) '*SAARC: Dynamics of Regional Cooperation in South Asia*', Vol. I and Vol. II, New Delhi, Kalinga Publications.
48. Upreti, B.C. (ed.) (2000) *'SAARC: Dynamics of Regional Cooperation in South Asia'*, Vol. II., New Delhi, Kalinga Publication.
49. Virendra Narain and B.C. Upreti (ed.) (1991), *'SAARC: A Study of Perceptions and Polic',* New Delhi, South Asian Publishers.

Journals:

50. Agrawal P., P. Sahoo and R J Dash (2010), *"Savings Behavior in India: Co-integration and Causality Evidence"*, Singapore Economic Review, 55, 2, 273-95.
51. Ahmad, S., Kelegama, S., & Ghani, E. (2010). *"Promoting Economic Cooperation in South Asia: Beyond SAFTA"*. Retrieved from The World Bank: www.worldbank.org
52. Ali, E. & Talukder D.K. (2009). *"Preferential trade among the SAARC countries'. Prospects and challenges of regional integration in south Asia"*, JOAAG, vol. 4. no. 1
53. Anasua Basu Ray Chaudhury, *'India-Bangladesh Relations @50 commemorating bilateral ties,'* Online Available at https://www.orfonline.org/series/india-bangladesh-relations-50-commemorating-bilateral-ties/

54. Ashraf, Fahmida, (2007), *"India-Afghanistan Relations: Post-9/11."* Strategic Studies, Vol. 27, No. 2, pp. 90–102.
55. Ashraf, Junaid, (2017), *"String of Pearls and China's Emerging Strategic Culture."* Strategic Studies, vol. 37, no. 4, pp. 166–81. JSTOR, https://www.jstor.org/stable/48537578. Accessed 7 Oct. 2022.
56. Asian Development Bank., (2007). *"South Asia Economic Report"*, Foreign Direct Investment in South Asia. Manila.
57. Bhattarai K. (2010), *"Strategic and general equilibrium models of poverty"*, Romanian Jounral of Economic Forecasting, 13:1:137-150.
58. Bhattarai K. and S. Mallick (2013), *"Impact of Chinas currency valuation and labour cost on the US in a trade and exchange rate model"*. North American Journal of Economicsand Finance, 25:40-59.
59. Bhagwati J. and T. N. Srinivasan (2002), *"Trade and Poverty in the Poor Countries"*, American Economic Review, 92: 2: May: 180-183.
60. Brandt L, D Ma, T. G. Rawski (2014), *"From Divergence to Convergence: Reevaluating the History Behind Chinaís Economic Boom"*, Journal of Economic Literature 52:1, 45- 123.
61. Borah, Rupakjyoti (2018), *"Japanese Foreign Minister's Bhutan Visit: Enhancing the Bilateral Relationship"*, Institute of South Asian Studies, National University of Singapore.
62. Casaca, Paulo (2020), *'The virus and the SAARC's awakening'*, SADF COMMENT Issue no. 174, Available from: https://www.sadf.eu/comment-174-the-virus-and-the-saarcs- awakening/ (Accessed on April, 11, 2020)
63. Cote, K.R. (2016). *'A Proposed Agenda for the South Asian Regional Standards Organisation'*. Jaipur, Centre for International Trade, Economics & Environment
64. Dalal, Saurabh.(2020), *"Relations between India and Nepal in covid-19 situation'*, Journal of Historical Archaeology & Anthropological Sciences, Volume 5 Issue 5, Available Online at : https://medcraveonline.com/JHAAS/JHAAS-05-00232.pdf, Last accessed on February, 03.2021.
65. Das JK Et al. (2015) *'State of neonatal health care in eight countries of the SAARC region, South Asia: how can we make a difference?'* Paediatr Int Child Health.
66. Dedola Luca, Peter Karadi, Giovanni Lombardo (2013), *'Global implications of national unconventional policies'*, Journal of Monetary Economics, 60, 1, 66-85.
67. Delinic, T. (2011). *'SAARC-25 Years of Regional Integration in South Asia'*. KAS International Reports.
68. Dhar, B., P. De, G. Das, and B. Singh. (2011). *'Expansion of North East India's Trade and Investment with Bangladesh and Myanmar: An Assessment of the Opportunities and Constraints'*. Research and Information System for Developing Countries (RIS), Ministry of Development of North Eastern Region and North Eastern Council.
69. Dogra, S. (2010). *'South Asian University: Catalyst for Regional Cooperatin?'* Institute of South Asian Studies.
70. Dushni weerakoon. (2012). *"SAFTA.'Current status and prospects"*. Institute of policy studies, Sri Lanka.

71. Fama E.F. (2014) *"Two Pillars of Asset Pricing,"* American Economic Review, 104(6): 1467ñ1485

72. Ghosh, A and P Sen (2012) *"Privatization in a Small Open Economy with Imperfect Competition"*, Journal of Public Economic Theory, 14, 3, 441-71.

73. Gupta Ashis, *'Afghanistan And India's Foreign Policy'*, International Council for World Affairs, Online Retrieved From: https://www.icwa.co.in/afghanistan-and-indias-foreign-policy/

74. Gautam, Prahba, RN, *"Formation of the Southern Asia Association for Regional Cooperation Federation of Critical Care Nurse'*s, The World of Critical Care Nursing, Vol. 12.

75. Hossain, S. S., and T. Rahman (2011). *"Trade Facilitation in Bangladesh through Simplification of Business Processes and Procedures"*. CPD Research Monograph 7. Dhaka: Centre for Policy Dialogue.

76. Hugar, Dr. Jayaprakash G and Kannappanavar, B. U, (2020), *"Research Contributions of SAARC Countries in Social Science: A Bibliometric Study"* Library Philosophy and Practice (e-journal). 4345.

77. Islam, Md & Karim, Md. (2019). *"UPDATE: A Research Guide on the South Asian Association for Regional Cooperation (SAARC)"*.

78. Isher judge Ahluwalia. (2013). "*Economic cooperation in south Asia*". Indian council for research on international Economic relations.

79. Jangir, Mamta, (2017), *"India and South Asian association for regional Co-operation"* International Journal of Applied Research, Vol. 3, Issue. 3 pp. 912-914, Online Available at: http://www.allresearchjournal.com/archives/2017/vol3issue3/PartN/3-4-36-354.pdf

80. Jain Romi (2005),*"India and SAARC: An Analysis*", Indian Journal of Asian Affairs, Vol. 18, No. 2, pp. 55-74.

81. Jayawardena, R., Ranasinghe, P., Byrne, N.M. *et al.* 'Prevalence and trends of the diabetes epidemic in South Asia: a systematic review and meta-analysis'. *BMC Public Health.*

82. Joshi Manoj.(2022),*'India's cautious return to Afghanistan,'* Observer Research Foundation, Online Retrieved From: https://www.orfonline.org/research/indias-cautious-return-to-afghanistan/

83. Jha Haribansh,(2021) *'A reset of India–Nepal relations"*, Observer Research Foundation, Available Online At https://www.orfonline.org/expert-speak/reset-india-nepal-relations/, Last accessed On October, 03, 2022

84. Kalor, S. (2016). *"Successes and Failures of SAARC"*. Indian Journal of Applied Research.

85. Karim, M.A. (2014), *"South Asian Regional Integration – Challenges and Prospects"*, Japanese Journal of Political Science, Vol. 15, No. 2, pp. 299–31.

86. Kaur P (2007) *"Growth Acceleration In India"*, Economic and Political Weekly, 42, 15, 1380-1386

87. Keshab Raj Bhattarai, (2016). *"Economic Growth and Development in India and SAARC Countries,"* EcoMod2016 9631

88. Khan Feroz, H. (2008). *"Security Impediments to Regionalism in South Asia."* Paper presented at the conference on "Does South Asia Exist? Prospects for Regionalism in South Asia". Stanford University.

89. Kripa, S. (2008). *"Regional Organizations and Conflict Management: Comparing ASEAN and SAARC,"* Working Paper 33 (Regional and Global Axes of Conflict), Singapore: Crisis States Research Centre, National University of Singapore, 12-15.

90. Krupa Vasani, *"Afghanistan's Re-integration in SAARC"* Retrieved on 25, September, 2022 from - https://jgu-dev.s3.ap-south-1.amazonaws.com/Afghanistans-Re-integration-in-SAARC.pdf

91. Kumar Rajiv & Singh Manjeeta (2009), *"India's Role in South Asia Trade and Investment Integration"*, ADB Working Paper Series on Regional Economic Integration No. 32.

92. Kumar, R. (2014). *'SAARC: Changing Realities, Opportunities and Challenges.'* Retrieved from http://www.die-gdi.de/uploads/media/DP_11.2009.pdf

93. Kumar Revanth.G & Pokharel (August, 2016), *"Appraisal of India's bilateral trade relationship With SAARC countries"* Intercontinental Journal of Finance Research Review, Volume 4, Issue 8.

94. K. Yhome, (2017), *"India's Evolving Approach to Regionalism: SAARC and Beyond"*, Rising Powers Quarterly Volume 2, Issue 3, 147-16

95. Leo O. Rose,(1987), "*India's Regional Policy : Non-military Dimensions'* in Stephen P. Cohen, The Security of South Asia, Vistear, New Delhi, p. 4.

96. Mazhar, Saleem, Muhammad. (2015), *"Issues of Good Governance in South Asia"*, Journal of South Asian Studies, 30(2): 127.

97. Mishra Vivek, (2020), '*SAARC's Resurrection: Leadership in the Time of COVID-19'* Indian Council for World Affairs, Online Retrieved From: https://www.icwa.in/show_content.php?lang=1&level=3&ls_id=4651&lid=3503

98. Michael Krepon, (2017), "*South Asia Confidence-Building Measures (CBM) Timeline"*, THE STIMSON CENTER, Retrieved from: https://www.stimson.org/2017/south-asia-confidence-building-measures-cbm-timeline/

99. Muni, S.D.(1984), *'Bhutan Steps Out'*, The World Today, 40(12).

100. Moorthy N. Sathiya(2022), "*Sri Lanka: Growing bilateral relations with India under President Wickremesinghe*", Observer Research Foundation, Online Available at: https://www.orfonline.org/expert-speak/sri-lanka-growing-bilateral-relations-with-india/, Last accessed on October, 03. 2022

101. Moazzem, K. G. 2012. Foreign Direct Investment (FDI) in Bangladesh (1972–2010): An Exploratory Note from the Host Country Perspective. In Bangladesh at 40: Changes and Challenges. Dhaka: Academic Publishers.

102. Nadkarni, Vidya. (2014), *"India and SAARC"*, Prepared for presentation at the FLASCO-ISA meeting, Buenos Aires, Argentina, July 24-26, Online Available at: http://web.isanet.org/Web/Conferences/FLACSOISA%20BuenosAires%202014/Archive/1226fcdb-083a-4d19-97bb-6f95edd84685.pdf

103. Niazi, Tarique. (2014).*"Ecological Disasters: The Political Economy of Floods in Pakistan."* A conference paper presented at World Congress of Sociology in Yokohama, Japan.

104. Nisha Taneja et.al (2013), *'India's Role in Facilitating Trade under SAFTA'*, Indian Council for Research on International Economic Relations.

105. Obino, Francesco.(2009), *"SAARC: The Political Challenge for South Asia and Beyond"* Economic & Political Weekly, Vol. XLIV, No. 9. pp. 118-125.

106. Pandian, S.G. (2005). *'Energy Trade as a Confidence-building Measure between India and Pakistan: A Study of the Indo-Iran Trans-Pakistan Pipeline Project'*. Contemporary South Asia.

107. Pattanaik, Smruti S. (2004), *"Indo-Pak Relations and the SAARC Summits"*, Strategic Analysis, IDSA, Vol. 28, No. 3.

108. Paul, Aditi. (2020). *'Regional Cooperation in South Asia: Exploring the Three Pillars of Regionalism and their Relevance'*. The Journal of Indian and Asian Studies.

109. Plummer, M.G. (2006). *'Toward Win-Win Regionalism in Asia: Issues and challenges in Forming Efficient Trade Agreements'*. Asian Development Bank Working Paper Series on 'Regional Economic Integration' No. 5.

110. Pramod Jaiswal (2017) *"Three Years Of The Modi Government India-Nepal Relations: Mixed Fortunes"*, Institute of Peace and Conflict Studies, Available Online at http://www.ipcs.org/comm_select.php?articleNo=5338, Last accessed on October, 03, 2022

111. Razvi Mujtaba (1986), *"South Asia and the SAARC"*, Pakistan Horizon, Pakistan Institute of International Affairs: Karachi, Vol. 39, No. 1, pp.120-127

112. Raza, H. A. (2012). *'SAARC Initiative for Regional Energy Cooperation and Current Efforts in Cross-Border Power Exchange'*. Paper presented at USAID/ Sari-E South Asia Regional Workshop on Transmission Operations for Cross-border Energy Trade. Thimphu, Bhutan. 28–30 August.

113. Rajeev Jain and J. B. Singh (2009), *'Trade Pattern in SAARC Countries: Emerging Trends and Issues'*, Reserve Bank of India Occasional Papers, Vol. 30, and No. 3.

114. Rahman et.al (2012), *'Regional integration and economic development in South Asia*, A Joint Publication of the Asian Development Bank and Edward Elgar Publishing.

115. Rahmatullah, M. (2009). *"Regional Connectivity: Opportunity for Bangladesh to be a Transport Hub"*. Journal of Bangladesh Institute of Planners. 2: 13–29.

116. Rehman, S. (2016, November 10). *"Second opinion-Foreign Policy in Crisis: Can Pakistan Overcome."* Retrieved from Jinnah Institute : jinnah-institue.org

117. Roshni Thomas,(2015), *"Radicalism in the Maldives: Should India be worried?"*, The Institute of Peace and Conflict Studies (IPCS), Online Retrieved From: http://www.ipcs.org/comm_select.php?articleNo=4888.

118. R.S. Siwach,(2004) *"South Asia Heading Towards South Asian Union"*, South Asia Politics, Issue II, March 2004, pp. 47.

119. Russell, Hasibul & Kouraklis, John. (2017). *'Impact of Foreign Direct Investment on Economic Growth of the SAARC Countries'*, The International Institute for Science, Technology and Education (IISTE).

120. Sappani Vijay, (2021), *'Charting a New Trajectory in India-Sri Lanka Relations"*, Observer Research Foundation, Online Available at https://www.orfonline.org/

expert-speak/charting-a-new-trajectory-in-india-sri-lanka-relations/, Last ccesed on October, 03.2022.

121. Sarker, Noor. Mohammad. (2013), *"Why SAARC is Less-effective? A Neo-realist Explanation of India's Role in SAARC"*, BILIA Working Paper – 01

122. Saklani, Udisha & Tortajada, Cecilia. (2019), *'India's Development Cooperation In Bhutan's Hydropower Sector: Concerns And Public Perception'*, Water Alternatives,12(2).

123. Shahid Kardar, (2011), *'South Asia—Intraregional Cooperation: The Way Forward'*, Asian Development Bank.

124. Shaheen, Irum. *"South Asian Association for Regional Cooperation (SAARC): Its Role, Hurdles and Prospects."* IOSR Journal of Humanities and Social Science 15 (2013): 01-09.

125. Sobhan, R. (2008). *'Bangladeshi Perspectives on South Asian Regional Integration'*. Paper presented at the Conference on "Does South Asia Exist? Prospects for Regionalism in South Asia". Stanford University.

126. Samadni, Zafar.(1987) *"SAARC Summit: Political Concerns Dominant"*, Pakistan And Gulf Economist, Vol. VI, No. 46, 14-20.

127. Sawhney, Aparna and Kumar, Rajiv, (2008), *"Rejuvenating SAARC: The Strategic Payoffs for India"*, Global Economy Journal, Volume 8, Issue 2.

128. Sidhu,W.P.S & Sandhu Rohan. (2014) *"Reinvigorating SAARC India's Opportunities and Challenges"*, Brookings India.

129. Singhal Soumya, (2021), *"Long Lost Lanka: Reorienting India-Sri Lanka Relations Amidst Chinese Expansionism"*, Social and Political Research Foundation..

130. Shrivastava, Smita (2005), "*BIMSTEC: Political Implications for India*", The Indian Journal of Political Science, 66(4): 973-988.

131. Smith, P. H. (1998), *"Public Diplomacy"*, Paper presented to the International Conference on Modern Diplomacy, February 12-15, 1998, Malta.

132. Sharma, Suman. *"India and SAARC."* India Quarterly, vol. 57, no. 2, 2001, pp. 99–120. JSTOR, http://www.jstor.org/stable/45073261. Accessed 15 Oct. 2022.

133. Taneja, N. and A. Sawhney.(2007). *'Revitalising SAARC Trade: India's Role at 2007 Summit'*. Economic and Political Weekly. XLII (13). pp. 1081-1084.

134. Upadhyay, Shashi.(1996) *"Pakistan Perception of India's Role in SAARC"*, South Asian Studies, Vol. XXXI, No. 1 & 2.

135. Udagedera, S. (2001). *"SAPTA Negotiations: Constraints and Challenges. In Impediments to Regional Economic Cooperation in South Asia"*, edited, Institute of Policy Studies of Sri Lanka and Coalition for Action on South Asian Cooperation in association with Friederich-Ebert-Stiftung, Colombo Office.

136. Weerakoon, D. (2001). *'Impediments to Regional Economic Cooperation in South Asia'*, edited by Saman Kelegama. Institute of Policy Studies of Sri Lanka and Coalition for Action on South Asian Cooperation in association with Friederich-EbertStiftung, Colombo Office.

137. World Bank. 2004. *'Trade Policies in South Asia: An Overview.'* Washington, D.C.

138. Yeats, A. J. (1997). *'Does Mercosur's Trade Performance Raise Concerns about the Effects of Regional Trade Arrangements'*. World Bank Policy Research Working Paper No. 1729.

139. Yhome, K (March, 23 2020), *'COVID-19 crisis and SAARC diplomacy'*, Observer Research Foundation, Available from: https://www.orfonline.org/expert-speak/covid-19-crisis-and-saarc-diplomacy-63598/ (Accessed on April, 10, 2020)

140. Vivekanandan, Jayashree, & Miklian, Jason. (2016) *'Bringing the region back in? ; Deciphering India's engagement with South Asia'*. NOREF Report, The Norwegian Peace building Resource Centre .Available from: https://www.files.ethz.ch/isn/195946/95c1cff7e24a7a923ea51ad89a5d9e02.pdf (Accessed on 30 March, 2020)

News Paper/Websites:

141. Anil Trigunayat, (2017) *'India and the SAARC: Implications for the neighbourhood,'* MEA, Government of India. Online Retrieved From https://www.mea.gov.in/distinguished-lectures-detail.htm?655

142. BBC News, "Article 370: What happened with Kashmir and why it matters", Online Available at https://www.bbc.com/news/world-asia-india-49234708/ Last Accessed on October, 05, 2022.

143. Bhattacherjee Kallol (February,03 2019), *'Buddhism gives firmer ground for India-Bhutan relations"*, The Hindu.

144. Embassy of India, Kabul, Afghanistan, 'India-Afghanistan Relations' Online Retrieved From: https://eoi.gov.in/kabul/?0354?000

145. High Commission of India,' India-Maldives Bilateral Relations', online Retrieved From https://hci.gov.in/male/?pdf1185?000.

146. Huma Siddiqui (October 21, 2020), *"Celebrating India-Bhutan ties: The Mangdechhu Hydroelectric Power Project receives prestigious award"*, The Financial Express, Online Retrieved From: https://www.financialexpress.com/infrastructure/celebrating-india-bhutan-ties-the-mangdechhu-hydroelectric-power-project-receives-prestigious-award/2110873/

147. India's Place in the world,(2021) Policy Watch, Rajiv Gandhi Institute for Contemporary Studies, New Delhi Volume X, Issue 7.

148. MEA, Government of India, (2017) *'Inauguration of SAARC Disaster Management Centre'* Available from: https://mea.gov.in/pressreleases.htm?dtl/28482/Inauguration_of_SAARC_Disaster_Management_Centre (Accessed on April 10, 2020)

149. MEA, Government of India,(March 27, 2020) *'Video Conference of senior health professionals of SAARC countries on the fight against Covid-19'* Available from: https://mea.gov.in/pressreleases.htm?dtl/32603/Video_Conference_of_senior_health_professionals_of_SAARC_countries_on_the_fight_against_Covid19 (Accessed on April,10,2020)

150. MEA, Government of India, 'India-SAARC" Online Available at: https://mea.gov.in/Portal/ForeignRelation/India_SAARC_2020.pdf

151. MEA, Government of India, India-Bhutan Relations, Retrieved From: https://www.mea.gov.in/Portal/ForeignRelation/Brief_Bilateral_Brief_bhutan_Feb_2020.p

152. MEA, Government of India, India-Bhutan Relations, Retrieved From: https://mea.gov.in/Portal/ForeignRelation/Bhutan_2021.pdf

153. Ministry of External Affairs, GOI, "India and Maldives Relations", Online Retrieved From'; https://www.mea.gov.in/Portal/ForeignRelation/Maldives-January-2012.pdf

154. Ministry of External Affairs, India-Bangladesh Relations, Online Available at: https://mea.gov.in/Portal/ForeignRelation/Bangladesh_September_2017_en.pdf, Last accessed on October, 03, 2022.

155. Ministry of External Affairs, GOI, Online Available at: https://www.mea.gov.in/Portal/ForeignRelation/Bilateral_Brief_pakistan.pdf, Last Accessed on October, 05, 2022.

156. Ministry of Foreign Affairs, Government of Nepal, *"Nepal-India Relations"*, Available Online at: https://mofa.gov.np/nepal-india-relations/, last accessed on February, 03.2021.

157. Niranjan Marjani, (2022), *'Continuity and challenges in the India-Maldives relations'*, Online Available at: https://www.wionews.com/continuity-and-challenges-in-the-india-maldives-relations-504965.

158. Omkar Dattatray/(October, 2, 2018), *"Indo-Pak dialogu*e, Online Available at https://archive.statetimes.in/indo-pak-dialogue/, Last scessed on October,05, 2022.

159. Panda, A (March 10, 2020). *"India Evacuates Citizens, Others from China, Iran Amid COVID-19". The Diplomat*. Available From: https://thediplomat.com/2020/03/india-evacuates-citizens-others-from-china-iran-amid-covid-19/ (Accessed April 20, 2020)

160. PIB, Government of India, "PM honoured with Bhutan's highest civilian award" Retrieved From; https://pib.gov.in/PressReleaseIframePage.aspx?PRID=1782810

161. PIB, Government of India, Retrieved From; https://pib.gov.in/PressReleasePage.aspx?PRID=1769254

162. PIB, Government of India,"Trade Agreement between India and Bhutan", Retrieved From; https://pib.gov.in/newsite/PrintRelease.aspx?relid=154916

163. PIB, Government of India, 'South Asian Satellite to boost regional communication' Online Retrieved From: https://pib.gov.in/newsite/printrelease.aspx?relid=161611

164. PIB, Government of India, Retrieved From https://pib.gov.in/PressReleaseIframePage.aspx?PRID=1857419

165. P. Stobdan, (2017), "*In the Tri-Junction Entanglement, What Does Bhutan Want?*' The Wire, Online Retrieved From https://thewire.in/diplomacy/bhutan-doklam-border-china

166. SAARC Food Bank,, Department of Food and Public Distribution, Government of India, Online Available at : https://dfpd.gov.in/saarc-food-bank.htm

167. SAARC, First Meeting of Foreign Ministers, (New Delhi), 1-2 August, 1983.

168. SAARC, Third Meeting of Foreign Secretaries, (Islamabad), 7-9 August, 1982.

169. SAARC Secretariat Retrieved September 21, 2022, from https://www.saarc-sec.org/index.php/regional-centres

170. SAARC Energy Centre (SEC), Islamabad. (n.d.). Retrieved September 21, 2022, from https://www.saarcenergy.org/

171. SAARC Summit. (2011). SAARC Food Bank: Will It Be Enough Broad Based, People's Campaign on 17th

172. SAARC Summit. (2011). SAARC Food Bank: Will It Be Enough Broad Based, People's Campaign on 17th

173. SAARC Summit, House 13/3, Road 2, Shamoli Dhaka -1207, Bangladesh.

174. SAARC Summit, House 13/3, Road 2, Shamoli Dhaka -1207, Bangladesh.

175. SAARC Cultural Centre Retrieved September 21, 2022, from saarcculture.org

176. SAARC TB and HIV/AIDS Centre | STAC Retrieved September 21, 2022, from https://www.saarctb.org/

177. Slater, Christopher L.; Hobbs, Joseph J. (2003). Essentials of World Regional Geography (4 ed.). Brooks/Cole Thomson Learning. p. 312. ISBN 9780534168100. LCCN 2002106314 – via Internet Archive. India now holds about 55% of the old state of Kashmir, Pakistan 30%, and China 15%.

178. The Dawn. (2016, September 28). *'SAARC Summit in Pakistan Postponed after the member states pull out'*. Dawn News. Pakistan: http://www.dawn.com.

179. The Deccan Herald (April, 17, 2020), *'Pakistan again boycotts India's COVID-19 training programme for SAARC healthcare professionals".*

180. The Economic Times,"*India Bangladesh Relations: Please do come and invest in Bangladesh:*

181. The Economic Times, (Aug 04, 2014), *'India, Nepal agree to review 1950 friendship treaty'.*

182. The Economic Times (March 20, 2020) *"India extends Covid assistance worth $ 1 million under SAARC emergency fund".*

183. The Economic Times (March 23, 2020) *'SAARC health professionals meet on Mar 26 via video conference to contain Covid-19 '.*

184. The Himalayan Times (April, 22, 2020), *'India donates 23 tones of essential medicines to Nepal to fight Covid-19'* Available form: https://thehimalayantimes.com/kathmandu/india-donates-23-tonnes-of-essential-medicines-to-nepal-to-fight-covid-19/ (Accessed on April 23, 2020)

185. The Hindu, 9 June 03, 2015),' National Knowledge Network to be extended to SAARC countries'.

186. The Hindu, (August, 12, 2019),"After Pakistan cancels Delhi-Lahore bus service, Delhi Transport Corporation follows suit'.

187. The Hindu, (April, 22, 2020), "Putting the SAGAR vision to the test".

188. The Hindu, (January 19, 2022), 'South Asian University remains without president'

189. The Hindustan Times, (June, 26, 2022)," Was cash strapped Sri Lanka duped by China in Hambantota Port?".

190. The Hindustan Times (April 20,2020), *'Afghan Prez Ghani thanks India for supplying HCQ, wheat amid Covid-19 pandemic'*.
191. Indian Express, 1st July, 1992.Bhargava, K.K., "The Maturing of SAARC",
192. The Indian Express, (November, 2, 2014),' Narendra Modi proposes special facility for funding SAARC infra projects'.
193. The Indian Express, (April, 13, 2018), "Operation Meghdoot: 34 years ago, how India won Siachen".
194. The Indian Express, (April, 11, 2019), "India cancels Samjhauta Express service after Pakistan suspends operations".
195. The Indian Express, (August, 26, 2021), ' India, Maldives to sign pact on Greater Male Connectivity Project'.
196. The Indian Express, (March 30, 2022". 'Explained: What's behind the new anti-India campaign in the Maldives?'.
197. India Today (March 14, 2020) 'Coronavirus: Indian defence medical team in Maldives to help deal with pandemic'.
198. India Today (April 09, 2020), *"Pakistan boycotts India-led meeting of SAARC trade officials on coronavirus crisis"*.
199. India Today (April 10, 2020), *'Pakistan pledges $3 million to SAARC Covid-19 Emergency Fund'*.
200. The Times of India, (September 1, 2017), "Siachen—the world's highest battlefield".
201. The Times of India (April 18, 2020), *'India's leadership helped South Asia to contain coronavirus so far, says European think-tank'*.
202. Wadhwa, Charan D.(May 08, 1991), *"Regional Blocs: Trade Opportunities for SAARC-I and II"*, The Economic Times.
203. Yahuda, Michael (2 June 2002). "China and the Kashmir crisis". BBC. Retrieved 22 March 2019.
204. Zaki, Ibrahim Hussain, "No India-Bashing at SAARC", The Economic Times, 3 March, 1992.